Bringing Strategy Back

HOW STRATEGIC SHOCK ABSORBERS MAKE PLANNING RELEVANT IN A WORLD OF CONSTANT CHANGE

Jeffrey Sampler

Foreword by Vijay Govindarajan

JB JOSSEY-BASS™

A Wiley Brand

Published by Jossey-Bass
A Wiley Brand
One Montgomery Street, Suite 1200, San Francisco, CA
94104-4594—www.josseybass.com

Jossey-Bass books and products are available through most bookstores. To contact Jossey-Bass directly call our Customer Care Department within the U.S. at 800-956-7739, outside the U.S. at 317-572-3986, or fax 317-572-4002.

Wiley publishes in a variety of print and electronic formats and by print-on-demand. Some material included with standard print versions of this book may not be included in e-books or in print-on-demand. If this book refers to media such as a CD or DVD that is not included in the version you purchased, you may download this material at http://booksupport.wiley.com. For more information about Wiley products, visit www.wiley.com.

Library of Congress Cataloging-in-Publication Data

Sampler, Jeffrey L.
  Bringing strategy back : how strategic shock absorbers make planning relevant in a world of constant change / Jeffrey L. Sampler.
      pages cm. – (The Jossey-Bass business & management series)
  Includes index.
    ISBN 978-1-118-83009-3 (hardback) ISBN 978-1-118-83008-6 (pdf) – ISBN 978-1-118-83007-9 (epub)
  1. Strategic planning. 2. Organizational change. I. Title.
  HD30.28.S254 2015
  658.4'092–dc23
                                                      2014024323

Printed in the United States of America
FIRST EDITION
HB Printing 10 9 8 7 6 5 4 3 2 1

Contents

The Jossey-Bass Business & Management Series

Foreword

Historically, innovations have originated in rich developed countries in the West and later flowed downhill to the populous developing world. But it is also possible for innovations to originate in poor countries and trickle up to the wealthier world. This is what I've termed reverse innovation.

I initially became interested in reverse innovation during a two-year stint as Professor in Residence and Chief Innovation Consultant at General Electric. At the time, GE CEO Jeff Immelt had put a stake in the ground to grow the company organically by meeting the needs and budgets of customers in heavily populated developing markets. As part of that plan, GE went on to introduce revolutionary new product adaptations—a $1,000 handheld electrocardiogram device and a portable, PC-based ultrasound machine that sells for as little as $15,000—created to serve rural India and China. By developing lower-cost end-user solutions, GE has been able to cultivate an entirely new market. Just as notably, these innovations have since been adapted and sold in the United States and Europe.

It's clear that if rich nations and established multinationals are to continue to thrive, the current generation of innovators must look beyond their own backyard and consider the needs and opportunities in the vast developing world. And the idea of reverse innovation extends well beyond just product creation. For starters, we see pockets of reverse *process* innovation springing up as well. Hospitals in India, for example, are transforming health care by performing open-heart surgery for $3,000 rather than the $150,000 we see in the United States—and not simply because of lower labor costs, but also because they have adapted standardized processes from assembly-line manufacturing to make the procedure far more cost effective. This type of innovation would be possible anywhere, but it's more probable in poor countries because it meets their needs and requirements.

The reality is that the future of growth and innovation is far from home—in places like Asia, the Middle East, and elsewhere.

Reverse innovation is any innovation that is adopted first in the developing world. This includes management innovation, a subject that Jeffrey Sampler knows extremely well. What he's done in this excellent book is bring my work on reverse innovation together with Gary Hamel's idea of management innovation to create a new model for understanding and using the latest and greatest management innovations from places as far away as India and Dubai. Economies such as these are radically different from mature Western economies, and they have radically different needs. Therefore, their solutions must be radically different. Based on the author's vast research and experience working with executives at companies across these markets, the "Strategic Shock Absorbers" introduced here form a tool kit of management innovation that was developed because the pace of growth and change in India and Dubai was so intense that the Western management ideas simply did not apply.

The tools and advice here present an opportunity, and a solution, for Western multinationals that are not only struggling with the ever-increasing pace of change at home but also looking for ways to compete with incumbents in developing markets. The companies featured, such as Arvind Mills, Dabur, Future Group, DLF, or Network18, may be unfamiliar but they have succeeded because of, not despite, the seismic shifts that have occurred in the Indian economy over the past decade. They have made the most of change and Jeff Sampler makes a compelling case that they set the standard in terms of innovative management practices that serve not only to hedge against risks and but also ride the ongoing wave of change and disruption that is common in developing economies.

The stakes are enormous for adopting the type of reverse innovations of management ideas described here. Today, rich countries and poor countries account for roughly equal shares of the global economy. But for years, growth has been far more robust in poor countries. Increasingly, understanding how success happens there is a prerequisite to continued vitality at home. In the transformed economic landscape, reverse innovation—including the management innovations featured in this book—is not optional in any market.

Vijay Govindarajan
Coxe Distinguished Professor
Tuck School of Business
Dartmouth College

Introduction

Bringing Strategy Back

Books, blogs, and business magazines feature charismatic CEOs and credit their dazzling success to bold strategy moves. Executives attend conferences about change and hire management consultants to oversee strategic reinvention. Everyone scrambles to uncover the next big strategy play in the haystack of operational imperatives. Why? Because in business we equate great strategy with great performance. Our heroes are the bold movers and shakers who can shift on a dime when it matters most and bring the entire organization with them. But this type of behavior is the exception rather than the rule. More often than not, strategic change occurs exclusively in reaction mode. Sales are slipping and market share is declining. Profitability is worsening. Disruptive competitors enter the fray and dethrone incumbents. Only then do we find that we are able to break the strategy mold and make bold moves quickly. But, having waited, these are often ill-fated attempts born of desperation, and they frequently fail or arrive too late to turn the tide.

Consider Kodak's famous fall from grace. For most of the twentieth century the juggernaut was the biggest brand

1

name in the photographic film industry, bar none. They were miles ahead of the competition in terms of innovation and industry dominance. But in the 1990s they failed to recognize the significance of a development that they themselves pioneered—digital photography. Although Kodak invented the first digital camera in 1975, they dropped the product for fear that it would threaten their bread-and-butter photographic film business. Even later, after Kodak realized the digital camera's significance, they failed to successfully capitalize on their early lead. Kodak declared bankruptcy in 2012, leaving analysts and consumers alike wondering how they managed to squander so many years as the market leader.[1]

In part, this problem of inertia stems from a change-averse mind-set, because until recent history we have been accustomed to relative stability, and the need for constant adaptation has been less urgent. But the larger reason has nothing to do with our poor appetite for change. Instead, the root cause is a dusty and broken process. In many cases, strategic planning does not work because the tools we use are seriously out of date. The five-year strategic planning horizon, for example, is a surviving relic from the previous age. Few today can plan five months ahead (not to mention five years), and so strategies die on the vine. As a result, executives in fast-changing industries are abandoning strategy altogether at a time when they need it the most. Consider the director of strategic planning at one of the world's top five technology companies who told me flat out: "Strategy is irrelevant in the current environment. In our case, success is about experimentation and luck." Few managers are quite so unequivocal in expressing their doubt and dismay about strategy, but many can relate to the idea that the tools we use are badly out of sync with the times. Our tried-and-true methods for planning are obsolete for a number of related reasons.

First, today's windows of opportunity close faster than ever. Over the long-term horizon, particularly in Western markets, we have grown accustomed to the luxury of comparative stability. Therefore, many companies focus on long-term opportunities to serve established markets that often change only slowly and incrementally. This is the type of opportunity that fits the mold of the conventional strategic planning process. It's predictable and familiar. Yet, increasingly, as we compete in fast-moving global markets, industry dynamics and new opportunities do not resemble the situation described here. Consumers are fickle and loyalty is fleeting. A product or service may succeed one day and disappear the next. As a result, there is a far greater need to react and adapt instantly to fluid opportunities. Most companies do not have this capability.

Figure I.1   Strategic Planning Is Obsolete

The range of factors ...

✓ Heightened level of chaos, change, and complexity.

✓ Intensity of competition, unpredictable market entrants.

✓ Windows of opportunity closing faster.

✓ Opportunities are shrinking in size and becoming more fragmented.

✓ Growth rates are volatile and uneven across markets.

✓ Traditional planning relies on past performance to predict future results.

Second, opportunities are shrinking in size and becoming more fragmented. Beyond speed and reaction time, companies are faced with the reality that many new opportunities today are relatively small (at least upon initial examination). Many Western firms ignore these opportunities because their strategic filters deem them unattractive. However, small opportunities can turn into something bigger, particularly in environments where requirements shift quickly and markets expand rapidly. Organizations need strategic tools (and a strategic mind-set) to target modest and often fleeting opportunities and accurately gauge their potential for growth.

Next, growth rates across markets are uneven and volatile year over year. In the West, GDP grows at 1–3 percent annually at best.[2] Whereas, in China GDP has surged at 7–14 percent per annum over the last decade while India achieved 6–10 percent for some time and then sunk to 4.7 percent more recently.[3] This means that a five-year planning horizon in the West in some years was equivalent to as much as a fifty-year horizon in parts of the East, because their economies were growing at up to ten times as fast. Thus, emerging economies in the East and Africa can't simply import strategic planning ideas from the West. The ideas must be scaled to fit their local business environment. Likewise, Western companies targeting opportunities in high-growth markets need to rethink their strategic tools and timelines to suit the local climate. In addition, as Eastern companies acquire Western rivals and vice versa, they must be in a position to plan for growth and retraction that is fast and difficult to predict.

Finally, the intensity of competition today is elevated and asymmetrical. One could make the counterintuitive argument that the last thing any company would want right now is to be visibly successful. Why? Because success attracts new competitors like hornets to honeydew. What was once a successful market becomes oversaturated; profitability declines and blue oceans quickly become red. Our strategic planning conventions simply don't factor in the speed with which new entrants rise from below the radar in both emerging and established markets.

The largest commercial real estate developer in India, DLF, is no stranger to this challenge. As Managing Director Ramesh Sanka told me: "Sometimes your size and strength can become a potential risk. It is a risk that comes with being the leader.... Once you are on that pedestal it is easier to mark you out."[4] Be it competing firms, new entrants, or even an organization's own customers and workers, the slightest glitch or complacency from a market leader guarantees a fervent response. This type of risk is difficult to plan for.

Taking all this into account, it is not surprising that the most basic principles underlying traditional strategy planning, including the five-year plan, are seldom valid. Traditional strategic planning is suspect, in part, because it relies on past performance to help predict future results. Anyone who managed through the 2008–09 recession (or the ones before or after it) will agree that extrapolating from the past no longer creates a clear picture of the future. One might even say that conventions such as the five-year plan are harmful to companies because they create the illusion of certainty. Lulled into a false sense of security, companies feel confident that major contingencies have been accounted for. With that, they view the task at hand as one of execution over adaptation.

This perspective has held true in past decades, but the extreme conditions in today's markets puncture the thin veneer of safety that traditional strategic planning creates. On the contrary, one-size-fits-all, long-range planning and prediction models have all but been laid to rest.

Where does this leave us? How do we bring strategy back and make it an ongoing process? If our tools for strategic planning don't apply, we find ourselves backed into a corner. Lacking alternatives, strategic change occurs in reaction mode. But the problem with reactive planning, of course, is that *it happens too late*. We find ourselves playing catch-up. The damage is done and someone else claims the competitive advantage. The challenge is to make strategic planning proactive and preemptive as a matter of course. That type of fast, fluid approach requires a mind shift, to be sure, but it also requires a new set of tools.

Setting the Wheels in Motion

The obsolescence of conventional strategic planning became apparent to me when I was researching cases in India. I was calling around to a number of companies four to six months in advance of my visits to schedule interviews. At the time, executives seemed universally hesitant to commit. I was confused, because in most cases I knew these companies and their executives, or was being introduced and referred at the highest levels.

I understood, finally, when one senior executive told me: "Call me two weeks before you arrive. I promise we will meet sometime during your trip and I will also arrange other interviews for you in my company. But, at this point in time I cannot give you an exact meeting date—I just can't see that far ahead!" Sure enough, when I called a few weeks prior to my visit, I was able to fill my schedule completely.

At that moment I finally got it. Scheduling time with an Indian executive six months in advance was asking the impossible. Their world operates at a different "clock speed," or rate of growth and change. At the time, shock waves were surging through their financial markets. Their tax rates and tariffs were changing. Government policy shifts were a regular occurrence. Their economy was undergoing rapid expansion. Considering the pace of growth in their sphere, I was asking these senior executives the equivalent of *can we have lunch four years from next Tuesday?*

That one stark realization set me on a research path that lasted over a decade. In addition to closely examining how dozens of top companies in high-growth markets were able to succeed amid turbulence, I also spent significant time in the company of a number of CEOs, senior executives, and heads of state in order to learn about their values and corporate customs. The research I conducted, often with colleagues, and the contacts I made allow me to present examples in this book that go well beyond the usual suspects.

More specifically, I collected stories and lessons from across India and Dubai. Why have I chosen to focus on these particular markets? The reason is simple: both countries at the time were experiencing massive growth and transformation. The planning challenges that exist in both places, then and now, are the effect of the corresponding growth and turbulence occurring on a regular basis. The level of development, the pace of change, and the ensuing unpredictability in the business environments made the nature of strategic planning there a test case for the rest of the world. All the growth that we have seen in India and Dubai, for example, occurred in just the last two decades. From an organizational perspective, they went from having a limited need for strategic planning to facing some of the most complex and fast-moving business environments in the world.

For instance, when India opened up its economy to foreign investment in the early 1990s, it witnessed a surge in consumer spending. This was partly a realization of the latent demand in the Indian market. Other factors, such as an influx of overseas money, had a noticeable impact. More basic changes were also under way in the Indian marketplace: changes in the pattern of consumption, a rising young population, consumerism, the globalization of their workforce, technological advances, and the rise of business process outsourcing (BPO). All of this made the Indian marketplace more dynamic.

The shifts that occurred between the early 1990s and the present day in India were across the board. The household per capita consumption expenditure increased 110 percent from 1994 to 2005.[5] The share of nonfood items in household consumption increased from 37 to 49 percent in that time, while that of food items decreased from 63 to 51 percent.[6] In the rural market, the share of nonfood items in the household consumption jumped from 34 to 45 percent, while in the urban market the share increased from 43 to a massive 57 percent.[7] These changes reflected the maturing of the Indian economy in many ways. Not only were Indian consumers spending significantly more, but they were also spending increasingly more on nonfood items. These many changes presented major opportunities, as well as extreme challenges, for companies in India and elsewhere.

Zoom in on 2005, for instance, when the United States lifted textile quotas. The sheer pace of change that was unleashed left Indian textile companies with no precedent to look to in a situation that was completely new and fluid. Consider India's largest denim producer, Arvind Mills. Growth at Arvind that year was not up to expectations; then, denim prices suddenly crashed due to new investments leading to excess manufacturing capacities in the market. China became a force to reckon with as it offloaded almost 40 percent of the world's denim supply into the international marketplace. With rising input prices alongside falling revenues, and with the literal doubling of competition and no one to blame other than the external environment, the underlying assumptions for doing business suddenly needed a serious reexamination. As we will see, Arvind Mills[8] owes its success after that to turning their every plan on its head and completely transforming itself in response to the requirements of the day.

Companies in places like India and Dubai that were caught ill prepared for such drastic changes—both economically and culturally—were left behind. Indian brands that were popular and rising before 1990 were suddenly bleeding market share. By the turn of the millennium many faded into oblivion. Risks of a dynamic marketplace include cost pressures, changing retail structure, competitive pressures, and human resource challenges.

Because strategy planning in India and Dubai needed to be modified under conditions of extremely rapid growth and dramatic transformation during this time, they present highly relevant case studies for Western organizations that need to learn the lessons of strategic change. DLF's Executive Director Saurabh Chawla explains that this anomaly is the reason why Indian companies are compelled to have strategic plans with much shorter time horizons compared to Western companies. "What would be a ten-year strategic plan in the United States would turn out to be a three-year plan in Indian context," explains Chawla.[9]

My focus on India and Dubai examples are intentional and intended to be instructional. The reality is that the turbulence India, Dubai, and other high-growth regions faced then (and continue to face now) have since become a global contagion. Turbulence and turmoil, expansion and contraction, growth and decline: all of these in rapid succession are the norm everywhere. The takeaways from the examples in this book, and the corresponding framework for making strategy relevant, therefore, are broadly applicable in any market. In addition, the cases and prescriptive ideas presented come together hand in glove. The cases each demonstrate all the ideas in my framework, as opposed to proving one piece at a time. This suggests two key insights. First, the findings in this book are robust and shared across a variety of industries, companies of different sizes, and countries. Second, the ideas in the model are part of an integrated system—that is, if just one or two ideas are implemented the results will not be the same.

The overarching message of this book, above and beyond the stories and prescriptions, is that we need strategic planning today more than ever. It needs to be an ongoing and adaptive process. With executives fully occupied responding to seismic shifts, surprises, and bumps in the road, it is crucial to have tools to simplify the task. The challenge for organizations is to somehow develop the capability to absorb everyday bumps and shocks in order to maintain operating speed and adjust strategy as the global environment continues to change. Like many of the management innovations of our time, the way forward begins with a solution from a different domain. It is retooled and translated here for the management space. Bringing strategy back is no small matter, but as we will see throughout this book, it is both possible and necessary.

1

Strategic Shock Absorbers

The fast, fluid approach that we need to soup up and accelerate strategic planning is not entirely unlike the performance features engineers have built into automobiles over time. In the case of cars, we have become so accustomed to certain crucial design elements that we nearly take them for granted. For example, if you ask someone: *why do cars haves brakes*? Most people will answer: *to stop*. If you ask a second question: *why do cars have shock absorbers*? Most people will respond: *for a smoother ride*. It turns out that both of these assumptions are wrong.

Cars have brakes so that we can drive faster. If the only way to stop is to plow into something or drag your feet like Fred Flintstone, then the default will be to drive very slowly. Similarly, cars have shock absorbers to enable speed. Before shocks, particularly in the early days, a car's frame would bend or break if it hit a bump at high speed. Thus, people had to drive slowly to avoid destroying the car. Shock absorbers enable cars to go fast and maintain their speed.

For executives, operating in a business environment that is extreme and unfamiliar is a lot like driving down a winding English country lane in very heavy fog. They cannot see far ahead. Perhaps there is a deep rut in the road or even a meandering cow. Driving under these opaque conditions, the reflexive response is to proceed slowly and almost feel your way along. Yet, this is not an option in business—the competition is too intense. Companies need to absorb the impact of unexpected events without slowing down or destabilizing the entire organization. They need to be able to react to bumps in their path immediately, before the impact creates a chain reaction and the wheels come off the wagon.

With constant change the norm, having a fast reaction time is crucial. There is a clear and convincing rationale for this. First, even small shocks have a cumulative effect. Companies are made up of a complex web of associations. They are global and multinational; connected in myriad ways to customers and employees; and they operate in an ecosystem where partners and competitors may be one and the same. With this interconnectedness, surprises that hit one part of a business or ecosystem can affect other parts in ways that are difficult to predict. The bigger the shock, the greater the potential for throwing off a destabilizing effect in multiple parts of the business. In addition, there are always new bumps just down the road a piece. When you cruise over a pothole and continue without regaining control, it becomes more difficult to swerve to avoid the sheep standing in the road or to veer around whatever obstacle arises next. In other words, stability is the exception rather than the rule. Companies need a means for adapting to environmental changes without slamming on the brakes every time. When the world is in chaos, strategy needs to be adaptive in order to be effective.

Through my research in fast-moving markets and surging economies I have found that it *is* possible to make strategic planning fast and adaptive. Over a period of five years, I worked intensively with colleagues inside twenty Indian companies in order to better understand the Indian approach to business strategy and to identify the key lessons. In addition, I worked extensively in Dubai from 2000 to 2008—around the time the United Arab Emirates was dramatically building its infrastructure and economy. The companies I examined in India and Dubai come from a range of industries—the media, manufacturing, air transport, government, retail, and banking.

The solution I found is what I call Strategic Shock Absorbers. Why Strategic Shock Absorbers? Because the capabilities that are part of this integrated framework allow companies to move quickly and fluidly, even amid massive turbulence. In addition, like the mechanism in cars, Strategic Shock Absorbers *oscillate*. They allow companies to move with the environment, contracting inward and expanding back again as conditions on the ground evolve. We will see that for each Strategic Shock Absorber time and information are compressed when conditions are grueling; and, when they improve, resources and options are expanded to unlock new opportunities. For example, as companies experience bumps in the road the Strategic Shock Absorbers call for lean operations that enable speed and precision. Then, when the environment stabilizes they expand—empowering people and preparing them to gear up for growth and new options.

Strategic Shock Absorbers create an ongoing capability for fluid strategic planning and execution. They work together as a unified system that is one part science and another part art. Used properly, they fuel organizations, such as those profiled in this book, as they work through varying conditions. There are four Strategic Shock Absorbers that work together in an integrated way. Separately, they create opportunities for organizations to pursue the new strategy plays described in this book. Together, they form a discipline that can be generalized to suit the needs of almost any organization regardless of size.

1. *Accuracy:* As a component of the Strategic Shock Absorbers, the Accuracy mode consists of a suite of strategy tools including *decision triggers* and the *strategic wedge*, which we will explore later in greater detail. In short, decision triggers

Figure 1.1 The Strategic Shock Absorbers

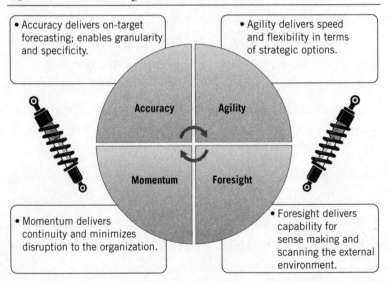

- Accuracy delivers on-target forecasting; enables granularity and specificity.
- Agility delivers speed and flexibility in terms of strategic options.
- Momentum delivers continuity and minimizes disruption to the organization.
- Foresight delivers capability for sense making and scanning the external environment.

Accuracy   Agility

Momentum   Foresight

compress options, thereby minimizing the time required to react in turbulent environments. The strategic wedge, conversely, expands a company's options by opening up new opportunities. In addition, because wedging opportunities are initially smaller, less costly, and less encumbered with financial risk, multiple people can undertake them simultaneously, thereby also expanding human resources. Both of these tools prepare organizations to pinpoint and seize strategies that accurately suit their needs at a particular moment in time.

2. *Agility:* This mechanism also compresses and expands an organization's resources and options—this time to enable greater flexibility and fluidity. Agility occurs in a variety of interesting ways including creating a *positive bottleneck*, which compresses information and funnels it directly to the right places in the organization. *Making strategy a bottom-up process*, a second agility tool, expands the people and options for creating and executing strategy. These particular tools, as well as others we will examine, come together to enable constant adaptation.

3. *Momentum:* This mode of operating equips companies to absorb shocks and bumps and retain speed. It is all about managing strategic inertia. *Focusing on the end as opposed to the means* (a compression tool) guides planning around pivotal goals and offers a wide degree of individual empowerment. Having *intellectual buffers, not physical buffers* (an expansion tool) builds up intangible advantages that lead to better decision making. These strategy plays create a mechanism that absorbs the impact of unexpected events, minimizing disruptions and enabling innovation and forward momentum.

4. *Foresight:* This last mode guides organizations to make sense of the future in two ways. First, developing *strategic assumptions* (a compression tool) serves to focus resources and attention on what the external environment looked like at the time of strategy creation. Second, systematizing *alternative strategies* (an expansion tool) guides companies to be ready to move on to what's next when the time is exactly right. Foresight brings clarity to opaque environments for the purposes of strategic planning. It is a lens for seeing bumps and surprises sooner in order to have a response at the ready.

These four components of the Strategic Shock Absorbers come together in a repeatable model that puts the power back into strategic planning. In the process, they deliver several notable benefits.

First, the Strategic Shock Absorbers enable oscillation described earlier, which prepares organizations to frequently adapt their strategy. As we will see, each of the Strategic Shock

Figure 1.2   The Oscillation Cycle
The Strategic Shock Absorbers create an oscillation cycle that compresses (information and time) and expands (the number of options and people) and back again.

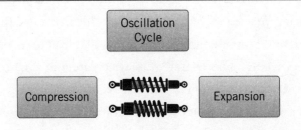

Absorbers requires people and precision (art and science) to put it into play. The science is in the strategy modes that are part of each tool, whereas the art is in knowing when to oscillate. In this way, Strategic Shock Absorbers balance people and process.

Over the years, a lot of management innovation has focused on the upside of empowerment. Although I do not disagree with this philosophy, I hope to present it in a new light. Strategic Shock Absorbers put people at the center of the process as opposed to at the margins. Individual judgment and creativity, after all, are crucial in times of change and turbulence. As Mahendra Agarwal, CEO of the thriving "FedEx of India," Gati Limited, told me: "In the present turbulent world the business environment is not entirely predictable. [Success] depends on [this]: How sound is the foundation of the organization? How strong is the management team? These two parameters are important in order to take care of any kind of uncertainty because turbulence will definitely be there."[1] Agarwal, having built a logistics and delivery business that has a reach of 99.3 percent of India, covering 653 out of 657 districts, knows something about empowering people to manage amid change.

Yet, my research also shows that in times of extreme change, organizations just as frequently need to *limit* people's involvement. This is where the oscillation comes in. Resources and options contract when surprises hit—because compression creates clarity. Later, resources and options expand again when we have clarity around the strategic plan. Knowing when to compress and expand is part of the art of management. It is discretionary as opposed to mechanical—but the Strategic Shock Absorbers act as an expert guide.

Second, Strategic Shock Absorbers help companies balance formal and informal planning. Oftentimes, companies are very good at creating structured planning processes that repeat year after year. These big picture planning and forecasting conventions are important performance management and measurement tools that work well in stable times. Yet, in unpredictable markets, strategic planning requires ongoing, informal, and unstructured interactions that are continuous and dynamic. And these informal interactions can end without ideas and intelligence being harnessed. The Strategic Shock Absorbers create a more structured place for these types of unstructured processes. Even more, they build a bridge between formal and informal planning and communication. It is this bridge between formal and informal processes and interaction that cooks the strategy stew faster. As we will see throughout this book, when brought together the formal and informal act as a catalyst for fast adaptation.

Similarly, the Strategic Shock Absorbers formalize purely informal planning conventions. Many of the organizations in my study maintain strategic planning conventions that are "matter of fact" because the uncertainties and risks they face are themselves sporadic. This creates efficiency gaps. To compound the problem, it is difficult to assign numbers, in terms of estimates and forecasts, when planning is so informal. The solution requires communication and transparency. Pete Goss, the British yachtsman and former Royal Marine officer who has sailed over 250,000 nautical miles in his lifetime, formalizes the informal with what he calls "bad news meetings." Predicated on fully honest and open communication, bad news meetings are just what they sound like—a safe venue for team members to come clean and solve problems. Goss, who famously sailed directly into hurricane force winds back in 1996 in order to save a fellow racer, builds a structure around these informal interactions in order to address issues before they can turn into catastrophes. Formalizing the informal adds structure but preserves the candor and creativity.

Finally, Strategic Shock Absorbers make strategy creation an adaptive process. Suresh Newatia, chief of strategic products at Gati Limited, explains: "Generally, we review [and adapt our] strategy on a monthly, quarterly, half-yearly and annual basis. One single strategy may not work throughout the year. As industry scenarios change, we have to modify our strategy accordingly."[2] That type of process for ongoing strategy creation requires specific organizational capabilities that Strategic Shock Absorbers help deliver.

As we shift our attention to examine each of the Strategic Shock Absorbers in turn, fleshed out and illustrated with a number of examples from my research in India and Dubai during their high-growth phases, the common denominator across this model is that strategic planning is more important than ever today, even as constant change makes traditional ways of achieving it obsolete. The framework and anecdotes are designed to make strategy relevant again and help organizations become dynamic. Bringing strategy back as an ongoing process is our best, and possibly only, chance to keep up with change and build change right into the strategy process.

The rest of the book looks like this:

Chapters 2 through 5 each introduce one of the four Strategic Shock Absorbers. They reveal the strategy plays that go along with each and offer cases and stories of companies that have put them to excellent use.

Chapter 6 examines the Strategic Shock Absorbers in action. It brings them together as an integrated model and shows how the approach enables strategic planning and execution that are fast and fluid. The chapter also demonstrates how the interplay between the expansion and compression modes yields a faster and more efficient organization.

Chapter 7 is about values—the one constant amid widescale change and chaos—and how they can act as a GPS for organizations trying to change while maintaining their sense of self.

Chapter 8 looks at management innovation from India and Dubai. It presents the approaches for shaping and executing strategy that have enabled organizations to adapt according to their own fast-changing needs. As described in the chapter, these elements are founded on a compelling and ever-present sense of corporate culture and an awareness of the changing external environment.

2

Accuracy

Creating Order and Transparency

For an omnipresent mass-market brand like Pizza Hut, ramping up business in China and other rising economies would seem to be the brightest bet for profitable growth. And, indeed, they've cultivated a large presence in many Chinese cities. This is true for McDonalds, Dunkin' Donuts, and Subway as well. Yet, although Pizza Hut and other YUM! brands (including KFC and Taco Bell) continue their march overseas, it is arguably more notable that Pizza Hut also managed to grow in the United States even following the 2008–09 recession when many of its competitors remained flat at best.[1]

Their secret sauce had everything to do with creating a discipline of accuracy around knowing themselves, their priorities, and the changing competitive environment. That is precisely what allowed them to make some bold moves that went decidedly countertrend.

To register growth in the congested domestic space, YUM! examined their options and decided to pass on competing with other popular pizza joints and fast food chains across busy US cities and sprawling suburban America. Instead, they analyzed alternative opportunities and put together a strategy to reach secondary cities in rural markets—cities that their competitors moved out of or passed over. From the outside looking in it appeared a risky bet: why should they succeed where others failed? But the plan was on target. With $5.3 billion in annual sales in the United States alone, Pizza Hut raked in more in 2009 than its nearest competitors—Domino's and Papa John's—combined.[2]

The management of YUM! made their distinctive location choices based not on the number of people in a city, as others had, but on the restaurant-to-people ratio. Driving across sleepy back roads from Houston, Texas, to Broken Arrow, Oklahoma, you'd have to choose between a dusty no-name pizza joint and an appealingly familiar and well-lit Pizza Hut. Which would you choose?

Beyond targeting hamlets that were dramatically under-served by national concepts, YUM! did their homework in these markets and made adjustments to their business model and value proposition. First, their analysis of secondary cities told them that price point was a critical factor to rural customers. They cut their asking price on menu items across the board, offering ten-dollar any-topping large pizzas, eight-dollar mediums on Wednesdays, and fifty-cent hot wings. They also simplified their online portal, knowing that long drives meant people wanted their order ready when they arrived. This pushed their expected web revenue to over the $2 billion mark.[3] Next, they homed in on what franchise owners needed to succeed. With that group in mind they downsized their floor plans, increased the visibility of signage, and put a much greater emphasis on delivery and takeout. These adjustments incentivized franchisees to open more restaurants, because lower fixed costs often enabled them to pay off stores in two years (which is unheard-of in the industry) and turn a profit much faster than before.

In short, thanks to their accurate assessment of market needs, as well as fine-tuning and focusing their own capabilities, Pizza Hut got the price-value equation exactly right for owners as well as customers. This allowed Pizza Hut to break new ground stateside after their close competitors had already decamped for foreign shores. That's strategic accuracy—finding growth opportunities and focusing on them. And there's more. YUM! used this same strategy to dominate in rural markets across China. Unlike McDonalds and the other leading fast-food players, KFC—the YUM! chicken chain—took the step of localizing their menus in China. Peering through the accuracy lens, YUM! found that KFC's product set would be a much closer match than burgers and fries or even their own Pizza Hut in terms of what locals were looking for. With that, they updated their offerings and aggressively expanded into second-tier Chinese cities. As a result they have dominated in dozens of Chinese provinces.

Internally, the Accuracy shock absorber delivers a clear-eyed understanding of one's capabilities and performance gaps. Externally, it leads to a precision awareness of the competitive environment. To get there, we will look at several implementation tools: *decision triggers*, management by *majlis*,

Figure 2.1   The Accuracy Shock Absorber

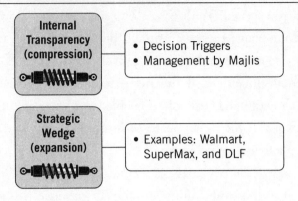

and developing a *strategic wedge*. Decision triggers allow companies to put a stake in the ground and focus on their most crucial objectives. Likewise, managing by majlis, a tool fashioned after a popular Islamic custom that brings people together to share ideas and information, helps organizations focus their agenda on senior management priorities. Although these two tools look very different in action, both are compression modes that yield internal transparency, whereas creating a strategic wedge is an expansion tool that enables companies to better know their external environment and seize emerging opportunities before they are apparent to others. In shock absorber speak, these tools use a combination of compression and expansion to create strategic accuracy amid chaos.

Decision Triggers

Imagine you are idling at a busy intersection in Mumbai, waiting for an opening to inch out into the chaotic rush of traffic. When do you move? How do you get in there? Traffic is thick, bumper-to-bumper, and proceeding briskly; no one stops to wave you in and there are no traffic signals anywhere in sight. In this environment you need a rule to guide your actions. This is what a decision trigger is—a rule that dictates actions and decisions. Individuals act faster because information is focused and compressed. In this case, the decision trigger may be: *When you spot a small opening in the line of traffic, move quickly to seize it before it is too late.* You would not pause to ask your passengers if they agree with the decision. By the time the question can be asked, the window of opportunity will be shut tight. This simple decision trigger allows you to proceed when you spot a rare chance to move ahead in Mumbai traffic.

The same idea applies within companies. Decision triggers limit options and create transparency and clarity around when and how to act. They are particularly useful in complex, chaotic environments where decisions must be made quickly without a lot of discussion. Compressing resources and activity around key actions equals speed. Not surprisingly, the Indian companies in my study all reported using decision triggers to guide their actions. For instance, DLF, India's leading developer of commercial real estate, holds one decision trigger above the rest in terms of importance and uses it as a guardrail during new business development.

A pioneer provider of grade-A office space in India, DLF[4] was, until their IPO in 2007, a family-owned business that developed some of the first residential colonies in Delhi. Prior to that, founders Chaudhury Raghuvendra and his son-in-law, K. P. Singh, consolidated their respective land holdings on the outskirts of Delhi in order to acquire property in adjacent states at a relatively low cost. With footprints at more than thirty locations in India, the DLF Group is at the pinnacle of the Indian real-estate market.

Yet, real estate is notoriously cyclical and vulnerable to pricing bubbles and the colossal corresponding busts. In order to hedge against huge property risks, DLF managers abide by the following decision trigger in securing the property for any and all building projects: *The cost of acquiring land must be less than one-tenth of the selling price.*[5] This decision trigger is a cardinal rule within DLF, and every employee understands its importance. It helps them hedge against risks and restrict potential losses caused by fluctuations in real estate prices. It also helps them act quickly and make deal decisions that accurately reflect DLF's overall goals.

Air Deccan

As a compression tool, decision triggers benefit companies in a number of ways. In the case of India's first low-cost airline, Air Deccan,[6] decision triggers helped them stake out their business and create a competitive advantage. In fact, the company's founder and CEO, G. R. Gopinath, a retired captain of the Indian Army, and his founding team crafted a matching set of two decision triggers that shaped Air Deccan and redefined the dynamics of the entire Indian aviation industry. The first decision trigger isolated their market segment. Even more, it identified their distinctive rationale for breaking into the airline business altogether.

Over the last quarter century, the transportation sector played a vital role in the development of India's economy. Some years back, global shocks such as the economic recession, terrorist attacks, the Gulf war, and the spread of epidemics such as SARS had a negative impact on the industry. However, the sector overcame these crises and subsequently recorded substantial growth. According to India's director general of civil aviation (DGCA), the number of domestic airline passengers increased from 12.8 million to 19.9 million during the period from 2002 to 2005.[7] By March 2005, domestic air traffic registered an increase of 26.8 percent from the previous year. And by 2011, the number of air passengers was 60.7 million.[8]

Clearly, there was an opportunity here. Yet, Captain Gopinath had no intention of competing with India's traditional carriers for passengers. Instead, his plan was to create an entirely new market for air travel by converting rail passengers.

India has one of the world's largest railway networks in the world, with 71,000 miles of track and 7,500 stations. As of 2012, it transported over 25 million passengers daily and over 9 billion on an annual basis, with revenues over $17 billion.[9] Yet, perhaps more interesting to Gopinath than total revenue was the passenger demographic: Upper-class rail tickets constituted less than 1 percent of passenger traffic, but they accounted for a significant *20 percent* of total rail passenger revenues.[10] Like the plan at YUM! to break ground in wide-open secondary cities, Air Deccan's fundamental decision triggers put a stake in the ground in terms of market. It was this: *Target cities with a substantial number of upper-class rail travelers that are underserved by traditional airlines.* Everything Air Deccan did as they built their business was in service of this guiding rule of thumb.

With this in mind, their target passengers comprised leisure, small business and corporate customers belonging to the middle class and cost-conscious customers of the affluent class. The carrier's airfares were comparable to railways' upper-class fares, and at times were priced even lower. This helped Air Deccan capture a vast segment of upper-class train passengers. For example, as of August 2005, the airline had succeeded in attracting approximately 18–20 percent of upper-class train passengers.[11] Notably, most of Air Deccan's passengers were first-time fliers. Thanks to this decision trigger, they were converting nonfliers into fliers, and occasional fliers into frequent fliers. This increase in first-time flyers in turn resulted in an increase in the market size.

In addition, Air Deccan's fares were approximately 30 percent lower than those offered by full-service airlines.[12] In order to provide low-cost fares and remain profitable, the carrier adopted a number of measures. It reduced its costs by simplifying operations through technology and by outsourcing processes that were not core to the business. The airline also eliminated extras (such as free meals) to its customers to focus on providing basic transportation services. In addition, they adopted the concept of "dynamic pricing" to optimize the load factor and the yield.

In order to make their strategy sustainable, Air Deccan's second decision trigger was a broader swipe at the same main objective: *Do everything in service of being a low-cost airline*. Air Deccan managers and employees lived by this mantra right up until the day they sold a controlling interest to the Indian beverage giant Kingfisher, largely because their decision trigger dictated the sale. (If they could not remain low cost, it was time to get out of the industry altogether.) And the two decisions triggers reinforced each other. In large part that is why the organization did so well. Targeting cities with a substantial number of upper-class rail travelers underserved by traditional airlines identified a large untapped market. The dearth of competition in these markets, at least in the early days, enabled their low-cost approach.

Their strategy locked up a large segment of the market and precluded others from entering. They squeezed out competitors who were unable to keep their prices low for an Indian consumer who demanded cheap fares above all else. As India's first airline with a "no-frills, low-cost" business model, Air Deccan's success also lay in the fact that the model was customized to suit India. They lived by their decision triggers in the following ways:

Optimization. High utilization of their planes was the first way they optimized systems and processes. One of the main avenues for achieving this was by reducing their turnaround time. In doing so, the carrier automatically increased its number of flying hours, which resulted in an increased number of available seats. In addition, to increase utilization rates Air Deccan meticulously systematized other activities such as aircraft selection, flight scheduling, ground handling, and route selection.

Air Deccan owed another measure of its success to the manner in which it planned routes. They operated from six bases located in the metropolitan cities of Mumbai, Delhi, Chennai, Kolkata, Bangalore, and Hyderabad and were connected by trunk routes. They followed the worldwide low-cost carrier strategy of flying on point-to-point routes. Therefore, they did not time their flights to connect with other flights, thereby eliminating waiting time in between takeoffs. This move contributed significantly toward reducing the carrier's operational and logistics costs. As an integral part of its growth strategy, the airline explored new route options on a continuous basis. These new routes were always those that were underserved by other airlines.

Matching different types of aircraft with the route requirements was another way they optimized. They used a smaller aircraft for several reasons—regional routes had lower passenger traffic, and most airports on these routes did not have the adequate infrastructure to accommodate larger aircraft. In addition, the costs involved in operating smaller aircraft on regional routes were lower as compared to larger planes. Moreover, the flight staff required for this aircraft was lower in comparison to that of larger aircraft. Finally, a smaller aircraft enjoyed lower sales tax on fuel, lower navigation fees, and no landing fees.

In service of their low-cost structure, Air Deccan also worked with a partner to create a new system for online ticketing. The IT solution comprised three significant parts—the reservation engine, the inventory engine, and the departure control system. The entire package was up and running in a span of forty days,[13] which by any standards was no mean feat. It sometimes takes years for airlines to get their IT systems operational. All of this enabled the airline to

- Realize an approximate 20 percent reduction in distribution costs
- Monitor yield management through available seat occupancy data
- Connect different geographies
- Improve cash flows via prepayments

- Reduce collection and administrative costs
- Optimize booking levels
- Sell tickets 24/7

Increased revenues. Air Deccan's careful balance of load factor and yield, described above, was one factor that enabled the carrier to augment its revenues. Its unique pricing model was another. In the dynamic pricing mode, seats booked well in advance had lower fares, whereas the seats booked closer to the travel date were priced higher. This helped the airline maximize revenues from ticket sales and maintain high seat occupancy. This pricing process was continuously monitored on a real-time basis and was governed by a defined set of rules. This involved checking prices against that of competitor airlines on an ongoing basis.

Yet, as the low-cost option, Gopinath and his management team were well aware that ticket sales alone would not be adequate to maintain or grow revenue. Thus, the airline targeted other sources to achieve this end. These included credit card fees, hotel and car booking services, and the sale of food and beverages on flights. Interestingly, one of their largest streams of revenue was in the sale of advertising space on seats, storage bins, headrests, tray tables, baggage tags, and boarding passes. They even sold ads, initially to technology companies, on the fuselage of the aircraft itself. Later, when India's largest beer producer, Kingfisher, launched their own airline, it was in part to skirt around India's ban on alcohol advertising.

Cost reduction. To make their low-cost business model sustainable, Air Deccan also innovated on the cost side of their equation—first, by using a smaller aircraft for shorter flights and for regional destinations. They also opted for a single fare system to avoid the additional costs involved in accounting and auditing processes.

This overall combination of optimized systems, increased revenues, and cost savings allowed Air Deccan to emerge as the third-largest airline in India in a remarkably short time. With decision triggers as their guide, they homed in on a new market and geared their offering accordingly. In fact, Air Deccan's success triggered the entry of several other low-cost airlines such as Spice Jet, Go Air, and Indigo, among others. These new entrants began to squeeze Air Deccan's margins. Gopinath was wary of these challenges, as well as of the tight regulatory environment and convoluted airport infrastructure in India that served as major bottlenecks in meeting the demands of the fast-growing aviation market.

In time, Gopinath realized that it would be an uphill battle for Air Deccan to compete with both low-cost competitors and full-service carriers and still meet its goals. In 2007, he sold a controlling stake in the company to Kingfisher Airline.[14] His instincts to enter the market in 2002 were right, and he also got out at the right time. Using clear decision triggers to delineate options, Gopinath and Air Deccan's managers read the needs of their market accurately and acted quickly as conditions changed.

YUM! made some very similar moves in the United States. They looked for markets that were small enough to be overlooked by major chains and large enough to welcome their name brand. Both companies benefited by compressing options so that their people could proceed in lockstep.

Creating Decision Triggers

Decision triggers are strategic guardrails that help organizations articulate strategy by compressing options. As we saw with Air Deccan, decision triggers put a clear stake in the ground in terms of creating a strategy that is simple and powerful so that people throughout an organization can make decisions that align with broad objectives. In a sense, decision triggers force management to define and defend their strategy. The act of stopping to craft decision triggers requires managers to do the work of analyzing the competitive environment and articulating how and where their organization fits in. Once that is established, individuals throughout the organization can act accordingly.

In order to yield accuracy, decision triggers must pass the test in a few different ways. First, they must stand on their own. In other words, they should be devoid of ambiguity and jargon so that employees can easily understand how to interpret them. Second, they should be distinctive. Distinctive decision triggers, like those at YUM!, help to set an organization apart and serve as a potential competitive advantage. Next, they should be actionable. By definition, decision triggers help organizations move forward in service of their strategy. Finally, decision triggers always require a careful analysis of the external environment. As a core part of strategic planning, they are only as effective as the strategy that they help to implement. With that in mind, they need to change over time as external factors shift and strategy is adapted or updated.

The most salient benefit of having clear decision triggers is the efficiency it creates in terms of enabling people to understand what matters most to their organization. That type of internal transparency yields not only engagement but also accurate, speedy decisions.

The Majlis System

Another means of achieving accuracy by internal transparency is illustrated by Dubai's "management by majlis" system. Majlis, an Arabic term meaning "a place of sitting," is used to describe various types of special gatherings among interest groups, be they administrative, networking, religious, or purely social. The majlis system, as it is used in Dubai, creates a semidirected open forum that managers use to share information and ideas across a number of stakeholders. If executed correctly, the system delivers a powerful transfer of information. Like decision triggers, it aligns actions with strategic objectives.

The Al Maha Desert Resort, for example, is an eco-tourism retreat that is part of the Jumeirah Group, a collection of luxury resorts and hotels owned in part by the ruler of Dubai, Sheikh Mohammed. Set in the desert just outside the city of Dubai, the perimeter of the resort is entirely enclosed to protect the endangered *al maha* (an Arabian oryx resembling the antelope) that roam freely on the grounds. At one point, the head of the Dubai office of McKinsey & Company happened to be visiting the resort, entertaining clients on a guided wildlife tour within the grounds. During the excursion, their teenage guide noticed a hole in the fence that surrounds the hotel and its expansive nature preserve. He got on the radio to his manager immediately to report that they had probably lost at least one al maha. To the surprise of the guests, within fifteen minutes Sheikh Mohammed himself was calling the young guide on his cell phone—asking questions and advising where they might locate the lost animal. The wayward al maha was found within the hour, grazing in the exact location that the Sheikh had suggested.[15]

One of the lowest-level employees in a country of 1.43 million was having a casual conversation with the Sheikh about a missing animal. Yet, what is relevant is not so much that this communication happened, but why it happened—because of the management by majlis system.

Majlis is a type of decision-making process not unlike an informal town hall meeting. The Sheikh has a majlis weekly and anyone from street vendors to billionaire businessmen can attend. In fact, it is not uncommon for a shop owner to stop by and mention a particular problem or concern. "My shop is being blocked by traffic from a construction site." As strange as it sounds to Western managers, the Sheikh invariably listens up and taps a close lieutenant to address the problem at hand. This gesture builds enormous goodwill, establishes trust, and creates an avenue for open communication. And when word gets around about the Sheikh's responsiveness, the goodwill is further magnified.

Management by majlis is not an exclusive tool for the ruling class. In the Arab culture, midlevel managers and even many private citizens have a dedicated majlis room in their homes. People gather and begin to talk about family or sports (if you are at Sheikh Mohammed's majlis you will likely be discussing racehorses) before inevitably getting down to business. Topics of conversation spread from one majlis to the next as members often attend several in a week. Through the cascading intelligence that occurs with this process, information moves freely and informally across the country from one circle to the next. It is a very organic and efficient system.

According to Suresh Newatia, chief of Strategic Products at India's express package delivery and logistics company Gati, informal communication and casual exchange of information is what guards the health of their business. "This is how managers can pass on what needs to be done and make sure that everyone is on the same path," he says.[16]

Management by majlis creates transparency. In this case, it means that the priorities of Sheikh Mohammed—like keeping the endangered al maha protected—are well known by his managers and lieutenants. Options are compressed because qualitative core values are widely recognized by everyone. In ruling a country or running a company, there are too many moving parts to have it any other way. When a protected animal escaped from the Al Maha Desert Resort, the people involved knew the Sheikh needed to be informed. Because of his knowledge of the area and the straightforward solution to the problem, it was faster to handle it himself than delegate it.

Think about your own organization. As a manager, do the people who report to you know your four or five qualitative priorities? At Air Deccan, every employee in Golpath's organization used cost and profitability as their decision triggers. If cost and profitability guide decisions, then the qualitative priorities may be to look for new routes or improve outreach to rail passengers. This is the benefit of majlis—identifying and communicating the four or five qualitative priorities that change over time. In this way, the majlis becomes a way to structure unstructured strategic planning—it makes implicit priorities explicit. With this, decisions triggers and majlis work together beautifully to create internal transparency. By design, decision triggers are formal planning tools, whereas majlis is the catalyst for formalizing the corresponding deliverables. By bridging the formal and informal elements of management, Strategic Shock Absorbers deliver accuracy.

In Dubai, the Sheikh's advisors are empowered to act on his behalf in many matters because they are fully aware of his priorities. At YUM!, managers knew that making franchises less expensive was an imperative. That is internal transparency. It gives decision makers and their teams clarity and focus. With options clearly defined, everyone is on the same page with an accurate understanding of a company's strategic objectives.

In addition, internal transparency is a two-way street. You may know your CEO's priorities, but does she know yours? Do you actively and effectively share new information with senior leaders? As a leader, do you know the concerns of the people across your team? In Dubai, the answer to many of these questions is frequently *yes*. The other half of the majlis benefit is the trust and goodwill that it creates. Shopkeepers feel empowered, if not entitled, to bring their concerns to the Sheikh. In being heard, they feel part of the larger team. They also feel obliged to provide important information in exchange. The young guide immediately reported the missing oryx. He was not concerned about backlash or blame, because in this system no one "shoots the messenger." It was his fast action that allowed the animal to be located.

Management by majlis is a key process for creating a shared understanding of strategic priorities. The accuracy it creates in terms of deliverables is one advantage but there are other performance implications as well. Majlis encourages empowerment, instills openness, and allows important issues to be addressed and problems solved quickly. That efficiency means resources are managed expeditiously and bottlenecks are kept to a minimum.

Finally, majlis is a way to build a learning organization. Qualitative issues require a more focused management perspective. They require trial and error, and majlis is one means for sharing what has or has not worked. Like Peter Goss's "bad news meetings," majlis is intended to be a no-blame opportunity to solve problems quickly. The ripple effect of two-way information sharing, like transparency in general, yields trust as well as engagement.

The Strategic Wedge

A second prescriptive tool for achieving accuracy is called the strategic wedge. Let's get back in our car waiting to pull out into Mumbai traffic. There are two successful strategies that I've seen used in India. One is to simply look straight ahead and then roll out into the busy crush of cars. This is what I call "might is right" driving—a high-risk strategy that works extremely well for large trucks, knowing that cars will stop to avoid being flattened. The other, more common, strategy is to find a small opening, pull out slightly, and wedge your bumper into the traffic. The oncoming cars must either stop to let you in or risk damaging their own vehicles in a fender bender.

Organizations in fast-moving business arenas use a similar strategy. They move into an available opening and start with a small activity or market, while constantly scanning the horizon for ways to expand their wedge. Slowly, that wedge forces open additional opportunities. In the West, we have become more accustomed to pulling out into the lane entirely and proceeding full speed ahead. We announce our intentions in Super Bowl ads and then take the market by storm—launching brands and even building factories in some cases. Yet, in the hypercompetitive, fluid global markets in which we all operate today, we need to take a different tack.

Beginning with small bets allows organizations to accurately size up an opportunity in terms of timing and fit. In addition, doing so offers latitude to make adjustments as conditions invariably change. If one particular idea does not pan out, you haven't committed your entire marketing budget. You can start anew. But if an opportunity *does* work, you can quickly expand resources and options to build on it. Wedging opportunities creates room to improve your position. And deepening an opportunity in this way comes about in large part by using the knowledge and contacts that the original, limited wedge activity provided.

This is how Walmart became the dominant retail player that it is today. Similar to the more recent strategy by YUM! to expand Pizza Hut, Walmart entered smaller Bible Belt cities beginning in the 1970s[17]—markets that at the time were considered unattractive due to their size. In Walmart's case, once their huge footprint was established in these regions, the discounter effectively locked out any local competitors because the ecosystem could not support another superstore. Their real goal was to get in before the other major players. They opened powerhouse smaller-market stores to build up size and gain leverage with suppliers. Then, with all of that clout, they were able to enter the major metropolitan markets and go head-to-head with established competitors such as Target and K-Mart. Their strategic wedge gave them a foothold that allowed them to roll right over the competition.

SuperMax

SuperMax, the second-largest manufacturer of razor blades in the world, offers another example of a well-executed strategic wedge. As a privately owned manufacturer, SuperMax was well-established in India and other emerging markets when multinational Gillette made a major play in the region in 2002.[18] Considering Gillette's deeper advertising pockets and influence with retailers, SuperMax was rightly concerned. Yet, they were able to best Gillette's initial entry into India by developing a strategic wedge prefaced on their superior knowledge of the local market.

Gillette's moves at the time reflected strategies that had worked for them in the West. Assuming the point of sale for razor blades in India occurred at retail outlets, Gillette used their muscle to try to dominate consumer shelf space in major cities. But SuperMax had a better understanding of the Indian market and used a different tactic entirely. At the time, most Indian men received their daily shave from a street barber: it was a matter of tradition in some cases and convenience or lack of running water at home in others.[19] Therefore, SuperMax positioned themselves farther upstream, aiming their strategic wedge at street barbers via their distributed sales force. The convenience and familiarity factor they brought in made a major difference to Indian consumers. Using their relationships with street barbers as a foundation, SuperMax established huge economies of scale and then expanded into retail with prices that were often half that of Gillette.

The wedge that SuperMax claimed also provided them with firsthand knowledge of the market, which enhanced their credibility with consumers. For example, the lack of running water in many small villages also meant that certain types of blades were ineffective compared to the traditional double-edged T-shaped razors of old. SuperMax designed their products accordingly.

As the India market grew, Gillette and parent company P&G (as of 2008) invested considerable resources in the region; not buying shelf space this time, but getting to know the market and customizing their approach.[20] More recently they offered a much simpler product at a dramatically lower price point, thereby appealing to what Indian consumers really wanted in a razor—value.[21] SuperMax was able to do the same job faster and more efficiently. They created a strategic wedge and expanded their resources and options slowly but surely from that first accurate foundation.

Wedge Opportunities

Strategic wedge opportunities are low-cost, low-risk strategies that allow companies to enter a market quickly and remain under the radar for a time. They are small enough to allow for flexibility and enable accuracy in terms of fit, but they are solid enough to learn from and build on. With this model, if your initial projections prove to be wrong, you can pivot in a new direction because you are not locked in based on a sizable investment.

Air Deccan created a strategic wedge involving air travel between smaller cities. They flew out of Ahmadabad, for instance, instead of Mumbai or Delhi as large standard carriers would. This small-market move allowed the airline to establish a toehold. Once they owned the routes from these "second-tier" cities, Air Deccan effectively locked out competitors because there was not sufficient demand to support multiple airlines. Air Deccan used their wedge as a way to expand into major cities in India. With planes flying from Ahmadabad to Mumbai, for example, they were able to leverage these routes to also fly out of Mumbai and into first-tier cities such as Delhi and Chennai.[22]

Air Deccan used the strategic wedge to expand revenues in other ways as well. Once passengers were on board, the carrier used that as a platform to conduct ancillary transactions. This included food sales and advertising to a captive audience. They also used it as a branding opportunity, for themselves and others, in terms of logo displays on the fuselage. In the end, these extras, as well as their smaller-city advantage, was why Kingfisher was first in line to buy Air Deccan in 2007.

With a strategic wedge, the initial move provides the toehold and market intelligence. To leverage that, simply look around for any direction to grow. The small size of a first move enables a certain amount of optionality, but building on that requires managers to be opportunistic—always scanning the environment. They need to be ready to use their position to adapt, as opposed to having one firm plan and sticking with it. Air Deccan did not envision a flying billboard business when they were starting out. It was a significant opportunity that emerged, and in the end advertising was part of what allowed them to keep their prices and costs under control.

The Art of Management: Accuracy

The companies examined throughout this book grew, through trial and error, in markets that were experiencing massive change and turbulence. Some were in high-growth mode, while others were simply in transition. That probably sounds familiar, as those same conditions of change and turbulence are a constant today in nearly every sector. The four shock absorbers described here are timely because they work together to create a capability for fast, fluid, and proactive strategic planning.

Peeking behind the curtain, the thing that makes Strategic Shock Absorbers effective is oscillation—the same dynamic that makes shocks effective in automobiles. Each of the four shock absorbers on most cars oscillate between two cycles, the downward compression cycle and the upward expansion cycle. During these cycles, hydraulic fluid and piston movement increase or reduce pressure in order to ultimately adjust to road conditions and control unwanted motions that can occur in a moving vehicle, including what is known as bounce, sway, brake dive, and acceleration squat.

Although no metaphor is perfect, the Strategic Shock Absorbers described here have the same oscillation effect. The compression (time and information) and expansion (of resources and options) act to help keep an organization stable enough to adjust and execute strategy while companies continue to move through change and turbulence. They allow for speed and stability.

Accuracy, the first Strategic Shock Absorber, oscillates using the strategy tools described above. As a compression tool, decision triggers allow organizations to maintain speed by making quantitative priorities well known throughout the entire company. They focus information and attention. The way majlis is used in Dubai, likewise, compresses time and information by creating clarity around appropriate qualitative objectives. It puts everyone on the same page with an accurate understanding of what management needs. Finally, the strategic wedge is an expansion tool that is well suited to deliver accuracy. Wedging opportunities expand the use of resources in search of opportunities. But they start small, so it is easier to see whether they will live into their promise. If not, it is possible to maneuver away and steer toward a different opportunity.

In this case, this oscillation of options, time and resources yield accuracy—enabling precision and control in the strategic planning process. The other Strategic Shock Absorbers we will examine have additional benefits that compliment this. And the oscillation itself provides additional advantages as well—from knowledge sharing and speed to enhanced judgment and increased transparency. The key is that it bridges formal and informal planning and communication.

Let's move on to look at these same compression and expansion dynamics and how they have delivered Agility at companies from Zara and Mahindra & Mahindra to Dubai's Free Zones.

3

Agility

Seizing and Repeating Opportunities

Louis Vuitton Fashion Director Daniel Piette described Spanish clothing and accessories shop Zara as "possibly the most innovative and devastating retailer in the world."[1] Innovative and devastating might be right, but you won't see Zara's designs on the runway at Fashion Week in New York or on the cover of British *Vogue*. The house does not advertise and their marketing department operates on a shoestring. Instead, Zara starts its marketing and R&D endeavors much closer to the sales floor.

The original "fast-fashion" house, Zara's business model is built around agility. For instance, store managers at Zara are trained to report back to headquarters weekly with customer preferences and dislikes: *We want sequins, not zippers. We need sweater dresses with shoulder pads, not A-lines, etc.* Zara uses this grassroots intelligence, along with proprietary analytics, to quickly design, ship, and stock stores with small quantities of new merchandise. And they get it there pronto. Zara produces items in close proximity to where they sell and their retail stores receive small shipments of new items about twice weekly. The overall design and production process takes only a few weeks compared to several months for some traditional fashion houses. Meanwhile, inventory levels at the retailer are kept low and turnover is brisk—if an item isn't selling it's banished from shelves within days.[2]

From Gap to Chanel, Zara also keeps careful tabs on what's selling elsewhere around town. When they see something generating buzz in the market they rely on imitation and offer the look-alike item for less. Zara's combination of fast, inexpensive, on-target fashion is a hit. Their tight integration of design, planning, and merchandising enables the company to be flexible and respond quickly to market needs. As a result, their sales were on a tear in 2013,[3] a time when much of Spain was teetering on the brink of economic disaster.

This approach works for other organizations as well. Karthik Krishnan, chief manager for corporate strategy and projects at Indian textile manufacturer Arvind Mills told me that they, too, plan in a rapid-fire mode: "In January the best prediction I have about my order book is out to February or maybe a bit into March."[4]

Considering India's booming economy at the time of that remark, it's no surprise that Arvind needed to continue to update their product lines six weeks out from sale. He went on to say that their entire supply chain from concept to invoicing ran about three hundred days on average.[5] Operating within the fickle fashion industry during the economy's high-growth phase incentivized Arvind to act fast and innovate. After all, they are cognizant that the business environment may change dramatically before any one long planning period is even over.

At the time, Arvind responded to uncertainty and market turbulence in two ways. First, they cut their planning and development cycle times by forward integrating fabric production into the manufacture of ready-made garments. In essence they became an end-to-end solution provider, supplying finished articles of clothing instead of raw fabric to US customers.

Gaurav Sharma, manager of corporate finance at Arvind, explains the change: "Earlier, a leading US brand would place a fabric order with Arvind, and the fabric would be shipped to the brand's nominated cutter, i.e., the garmenting factory. The cutter could be in Sri Lanka or Bangladesh or in South America or Africa. Now we use our own fabric and garment factory in Bangalore. Within three days the fabric is sent to Bangalore. The garments are prepared there and the finished items are supplied directly to the customer."[6]

Second, Arvind assembled a crackerjack team of specialists to look at trends and consider new product development. As part of that they have experts eyeballing processes across the manufacturing cycle—spinners, dyers, weavers, and specialists in finishing and washing. Their task is to ensure that Arvind is using the latest intelligence and technology to remain fast and flexible.

Overall, both Arvind and Zara have pioneered a very complex and innovative method for remaining in sync with changing fashion trends. According to Arvind executives, an attendant element of a fast-acting culture is to proceed with a dash of caution because fashion evolves constantly. After all, what you see in the stores today may not be what you see tomorrow.[7]

In the face of uncertainty around the world, companies need to be in a position to react quickly to conditions in flux. They need agility. Think about driving a sports car versus an American family car from the 1960s or '70s. The sports car is clearly more agile. Still, many companies are designed like the family cars of old—big, comfortable cruising machines that perform best under stable conditions. If they roll over a bump while driving fast the transmission is likely to drop out of the bottom. The Agility shock absorber gives them the tools to keep that from ever happening.

V. C. Agerwal, a vice president at New Delhi's Moser Baer, one of the world's largest manufacturers of optical storage media like CDs and DVDs, put it this way: "We operate in an industry characterized by rapid growth and short market and product cycles. Unlike conventional manufacturing industries, we measure change in weeks and months, not in years. But our perspective of change extends beyond the physical to include mind-sets too. Our managers accept and imbibe change as a daily occurrence. We proactively adapt to change rather than be challenged or worried by it."[8]

Figure 3.1 The Agility Shock Absorber

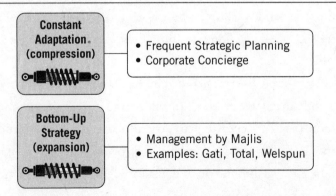

In order to create a capability for agility, I will introduce two concepts that make up this tool in the Strategic Shock Absorbers: *Constant Adaptation* and *Strategy as a Bottom-Up Process*. As we will see, this shock absorber contains both compression tools—reducing the time in between strategic planning cycles, and expansion tools—bringing many more people into the planning process and increasing options. By oscillating between the compression and expansion parts of Agility, companies will develop a greater capability for speed and flexibility in their strategic planning.

Constant Adaptation

As Arvind Mills and Zara illustrate, a primary ingredient of agility is the ability to respond quickly to challenges in the environment. Constant adaptation is one way to make that happen. At Zara in particular, constant adaptation happens through the rapid design and roll out of new fashion. Time is compressed and planning occurs faster and more frequently. In Zara's case, they use frequent product planning cycles to record growth in an industry that is largely flat. But the need for constant adaption is relevant far beyond the fickle world of fashion.

Moore's Law is one famous way to examine the rapid pace of change and how it affects businesses of every stripe. This axiom of technology says that the number of transistors stored on integrated circuits doubles every two years, thereby exponentially increasing the power of computer chips while the cost halves in that same two-year period. As processing power, digital memory capacity, and even the pixels in digital cameras improves, so too does the pace of performance in computer programs and algorithms that track data for everything from financial transactions and strategy to global transportation systems and air traffic control.

The world is moving faster and constant adaption is one way that companies can keep up with technological progress, consumer demand, and global competition. In terms of how to achieve constant adaptation, there are two ways to consider: *Frequent Planning Cycles* and *the Corporate Concierge*. As components of this Strategic Shock Absorber, frequent planning cycles compress time, whereas a corporate concierge compresses information. Both of these tools allow companies to adapt faster and build agility into their processes.

Frequent Planning Cycles

At Zara, they plan and produce clothes and accessories in two weeks or less—bypassing formal market research,[9] long-range financial modeling, and countless meetings with executives manning flip charts and smart boards. They make decisions in less time based on current data and change frequently when they veer off course.

The "fast-fashion footwear" business Charles & Keith is a lot like Zara in this way. One of the key factors in the brand's success is its frequent product planning. For instance, some twenty styles are rolled out each week to keep its customers interested.[10] Again, the time from idea to rollout is compressed. The Singapore-based business, owned in part by LVMH, has weekly calls between regional managers and the home office in order to upload local insights and product ideas that might be of interest to the wider business.

Most traditional companies follow a three- to five-year strategic planning cycle, and they conduct financial planning reviews annually. Budgeting goals are increased or decreased each year depending upon the prior year's performance. Products are plotted out well in advance. This is the norm in most large Western companies. Yet, opportunities and challenges aren't cyclical and they can't be planned by the calendar. Established financial planning is time consuming, costly, and largely obsolete in today's fast-moving world where the window available to make crucial decisions is compressed. Consider 2009: the planning cycle for the year began with dramatic market changes that rendered goals and budgets obsolete before the first quarter had ended.

In addition, focusing on performance goals that are months or years away creates tunnel vision, making it impossible to respond to important signals from the market. Agility entails a fast, flexible response to the external environment. When YUM! ran out of runway to expand in large US cities they shifted gears and realigned their domestic business model to reach wide-open smaller markets across the Midwest.

More than halfway across the world, the Indian automaker Mahindra & Mahindra is an organization that takes frequent planning to new heights. They have honed their capability to change on the fly because they have compressed their planning cycles into a *monthly* exercise. This is not the way GM, Ford, or even Toyota is set up to operate. But at Mahindra & Mahindra, constant adaptation (not just a readjustment of a five-year plan) is a way to respond to a changing world. They compress the time from idea to action. Initially, frequent planning might seem radical or even wasteful, but for any company experiencing market turbulence this process can be a powerful means for becoming responsive to the external environment. There is no way to shut out signals from the market when you have built them into the process.

For example, in 2004, India's economy was experiencing a 7.9 percent GDP growth.[11] Consumers in India were buying cars at a fast clip and Mahindra & Mahindra was able to very quickly step up production in response to demand. In 2010, growth in India rose to 10 percent, but in 2013 it fell closer to 4.5 percent.[12] Frequent strategic planning enabled Mahindra & Mahindra to respond in real time to wild swings and remain at the top of the auto industry in India. They have the capability to compress their planning cycle and adjust production more frequently than their competitors. With auto sales down, Mahindra has decreased production and is moving resources to focus on alliances in other parts of the world. When India picks up again, Mahindra is likely to be a first responder—because their strategic planning process allows for it. That is compression.

How effective is Mahindra's mode of operating? A few years back a close colleague of mine was in Mahindra's showroom in Mumbai to place an order for an SUV when he noticed there was no full-sized rear seat cup holder in the model he wanted. My colleague complained, but he nevertheless ordered the car. When the car arrived eight weeks later—sure enough, the full-size cup holder was in place in the back. Another acquaintance of mine had a similar experience in Hyderabad. She needed more seating space but placed an order despite the lack of a third-row option. Six weeks later she received a car with the third row in place.

Like the system at Zara, the salespeople at Mahindra & Mahindra are trained to listen to customer ideas and report back to headquarters. If management believes the idea is reasonable, they have the ability to quickly integrate new features into their manufacturing and production process. In India, having a chauffeur is extremely common, and professionals spend most of their time riding in the back. Therefore, the rear-seat cup holder made excellent sense. Likewise, families in India live together in multigenerational homes. Again, a third-row option is reasonable and Mahindra made it a reality in a matter of weeks.

Producing cars is arguably far more complex than making clothes, yet frequent strategic planning has made agility a part of Mahindra's DNA. Without this capability to compress their response time, Mahindra would have a difficult time keeping up with the fast changes in India and across the world.

The Corporate Concierge

Mahindra & Mahindra captured ideas directly from customers and used them to keep up with fast-changing consumer needs. Without a way to capture ideas and trends, organizations that are large and dispersed can suffer when information escapes without a trace because there is no existing process to capture it. One way to isolate ideas and funnel customer needs is to create a positive bottleneck of sorts. At Zara, customer intelligence is captured on the sales floor and delivered directly to the design team.

A different way to approach this is by creating a "corporate concierge." The corporate concierge—a compression tool that optimizes relationships with external partners (customers, suppliers, and vendors)—puts more power into each interaction by centralizing knowledge and channeling it up the chain of command. One analogy is the Panama Canal. What is the best way to sail from New York to San Francisco? On a direct course. Before the canal was built, a ship sailing from ports in New York to San Francisco had to chart a course around Cape Horn, the outermost point of South America. This trip took over two months. After the canal was completed, approximately eight thousand miles and eight weeks were eliminated from the excursion. Like the Panama Canal, a corporate concierge creates a direct line—from external stakeholders to management and back again—that is a direct and effective way to get from point A to point B. If a partner or customer needs something quickly, why not make it easy? If management wants to access market information, why not create a direct line?

A corporate concierge model is something that worked well on a grand scale during Dubai's turbulent high-growth phase. Like India, Dubai experienced massive growth and waves of accelerated change and turbulence. In 2006, the economy of Dubai was valued at $46 billion, and by 2008 the gross domestic product had shot up to $82.11 billion.[13] Yet, even before that massive growth, Dubai's free zones were attracting foreign investment. The challenge faced by Dubai's government beginning around 2000 was to bring businesses in quickly to fuel their expanding economy.

The catalyst for this business building was the creation of Dubai's free zones—industrial hubs organized by sector. These zones had advantages built into them for businesses, such as preferential taxation and customs status, as well as an infrastructure designed to meet sector-specific needs.

Dubai's Internet City, for example, was launched in October 2000 to cater to technology companies. By 2008, Microsoft, Oracle, Cisco, Hewlett-Packard, and IBM were among nine hundred or more companies in residence as part of a technology cluster.[14] Today, Facebook, Yahoo!, and LinkedIn are also part of the ecosystem. Beyond the technological infrastructure, much of the accelerated value for the tenant companies comes from the concierge services offered in these zones. For example, any logistical or bureaucratic problem or requirement that comes up for a guest company is managed through a single point of contact. The corporate concierge guarantees items such as the procurement of work permits for foreign workers within twenty-four hours. They also resolve thorny business questions and handle nonbusiness logistics.[15]

Yet, perhaps even more interesting and useful, the corporate concierge has important benefits and by-products for an organization—the country of Dubai in this case. One dedicated and centralized external-facing function, like the corporate concierge, provides a direct line to external stakeholders. Organizations can become bogged down responding to crises and internal dilemmas and they miss crucial signals from the market. This is especially problematic in times of fast change when attention is divided. One executive I know in the shipping business in Sydney prefers to have an office right on the port because it helps to focus his sights on business. How do you know what your suppliers/partners/clients need and want? With the corporate concierge they can tell you directly. How did Dubai know that twenty-four-hour visas were a priority? Their clients told them, and Dubai responded accordingly. The corporate concierge is a compression mechanism (streamlines the flow of information) that creates a portal to the outside world.

Other free zones in Dubai include Dubai Media City and Dubai Medical City. Each cluster has one or more anchor tenants to establish credibility. The Medical City, for example, hosts a Harvard Medical School facility. Media City hosts Bertelsmann and CNN. In addition, the infrastructure and ethos in these zones encouraged the sharing among companies of not just resources but also ideas. They were built to encourage and systematize synergy. And there is often as much business *between* the tenants as there was conducted from them to the outside world.

For Dubai, the corporate concierge model has several advantages for the principality and its citizens. Notably, it exposes the people and companies of Dubai to ideas and innovation from leading organizations around the world. If Microsoft or another company in Internet City launches a new product or service, Dubai entrepreneurs and executives have a front-row seat. They can reach out directly to someone at Microsoft who is operating in the same time zone. Beyond that close connection to innovation, it also exposes Dubai UAE citizens to world-class business practices and skills that they keep in the emirate. It is a way to improve and modernize their workforce as a nation state. For instance, the head of each development in Dubai sits down with their concierge team weekly in order to ask about issues and trends. The concierge structure, then, acts as a funnel to capture useful intelligence. Likewise, this approach can allow any organization to get an integrated view of their rapidly changing environment.

Although it looks a little different internally, the corporate concierge model can create a valuable integrating mechanism within an organization. It offers a strategic purview of the landscape that executives need to connect the dots on trends and disparate signals. This is yet another way the Strategic Shock Absorbers formalize the informal and creates a bridge between two separate worlds. To some, this concept of a concierge may be reminiscent of the shared service center, which sometimes amounts to a backwater of back-office tasks. Customer service and human resources departments, for example, are oftentimes centralized, and they are seldom known for speed or innovation. But when structured and managed appropriately, the corporate concierge is a strong enabler of innovation, allowing ideas to flow in more easily from the outside.

Unlike customer service and HR, the corporate concierge is focused on bringing intelligence into an organization in a B2B fashion. Just as Zara's B2C retail model enables fast planning via individual feedback, the corporate concierge gives management an up-close look at stakeholders that may be scattered around the globe. As in the case of my friend with an office overlooking Sydney Harbour, having immediate access to the external business makes strategic planning easier because it delivers fresh insights directly. When the port is empty, you see that. When it is bustling with energy, it's right there.

The corporate concierge provides a focused point of contact and oversight for customers and partners or stakeholders. It also creates a bird's-eye view of emerging trends and issues. For instance, if a technology company uses a corporate concierge to handle external alliances, it can also use the concierge to determine which trends the market is betting on. How important is cloud computing or big data? Internally or externally, the power of a corporate concierge is in strategic insight and focus. Looking historically at major disasters, such as the Pearl Harbor or 9/11 attacks, investigations invariably reported that signals existed, foreshadowing impending events. Why did they fail to trigger action? Because the signals were so diffused and dispersed that no one understood their frequency until it was too late. The corporate concierge can be an integrating mechanism to allow organizations to recognize key trends and adapt to change sooner because they are more certain to receive and likely to understand the signals.

Creating a Corporate Concierge

How easy is it for outsiders to work with your company? Do you have a system in place to capture ideas and value created by partners and clients? Small entrepreneurial companies tend to home in on opportunities as a matter of course. It happens informally because networks are strong and people's jobs overlap more or less by chance. However, in governments, and large companies with vast numbers of employees separated by multiple silos, intelligence gets lost in translation or distorted like in the children's game known as telephone.

A corporate concierge eliminates some of the distortion by creating a job function for identifying trends. What makes this tool effective is the systematic interaction between managers and stakeholders. The interaction delivers feedback and ideas from stakeholders and allows managers to act on them. Without a corporate concierge, valuable ideas are never captured. In addition, the corporate concierge positions the manager to support innovation (as a catalyst for change) as opposed to being responsible for creating the innovation.

A large US-based communications company I work with makes the corporate concierge approach effective by placing veteran employees in "ambassador" roles, locking in their knowledge and experience right around the time they might ordinarily think to retire. This is their way not only to keep expertise in the company longer, but also to make the most of the trust these ambassadors have cultivated over the years with external partners, large customers, and even employees internally.

Turbulence and change are everywhere—not just in India and Dubai. Creating a corporate concierge—a single point of interaction for dealing with outside companies and analyzing key intelligence—improves competitiveness by channeling important information to the right places. It is also a powerful catalyst for cross-pollination, helping to create synergies between business units and building bridges across silos.

When all new ideas, potential alliances, and so forth filter through a focused team of experienced individuals charged with channeling intelligence to the rest of the organization, decision makers can rely on their informed perspective to make better choices. Remember Nokia? They lost to Apple in the smartphone wars because they were focusing on colorful cases when their customers wanted intelligent operating systems.

The corporate concierge is a compression tool that funnels insights and intelligence from the market directly to managers. That intel is exactly what companies can use to lay the groundwork for frequent planning that is fast and responsive. These two tools—frequent planning (compresses time) and corporate concierge (compresses information)—make up the Constant Adaptation half of the Agility shock absorber. The second half is enabled though an expansion tool: Bottom-Up Strategic Planning.

Making Strategy a Bottom-Up Process

Strategy has traditionally been a process driven from the top down. A few senior executives in the strategy department are charged with looking into the future and developing a plan. Everyone else sees the plan in its polished form when it's past the point of no return. But it is the people who witness the specter of change (and experience it firsthand) who are best equipped to plan a response. These people often reside at the lower tiers in the organization—closest to the front line. Bottom-up planning by people with their eyes on change has been the case in high-tech start-ups where, by design, there is a lack of hierarchy and everyone works on the front line. But my research in India and Dubai shows that it also happens in many other types of companies.

Gati Limited, India's version of Federal Express, offers a look at a large organization that believes bottom-up planning is one of the reasons they succeed.[16]

Mahendra Agarwal, a mechanical engineer and entrepreneur who studied the US cargo industry in business school in the States, conceived Gati's business plan. At the time, his family owned TCI—one of the top three transport companies in India. In effect, Agarwal wanted to modernize his family's otherwise successful transport business with an emphasis on systems and logistics. Gati was designed to be the first cargo management company in India to offer time-definite door-to-door delivery and a money-back guarantee. With that as the goal, Agarwal launched Gati in 1989 as a TCI subsidiary with four locations spanning across southeast India. In this case, the bottom-up approach was ideal, if not crucial, because the company was so geographically spread out.

Gati's main office, home base for many of their senior leaders, is located in Secunderabad in east India; their Singapore location is Gati's international business hub. The company has additional offices in Hong Kong, China, Thailand, and Dubai. Their domestic operations are divided into zones: North, East, West, South, and Central India. Because the scope of operations stretches across the country, the zones are decentralized. Managers in each are authorized to make operational decisions and all have their own functional head; Suresh Newatia, chief of Strategic Products at Gati, says that day-to-day decisions in each zone are made by these functional heads.[17] Empowerment is explicit at all levels, and they plan independently within certain predefined boundaries. According to executives, there is a lot of free hand at Gati and the managing director plays more of a big-picture strategic and sometimes a mentor role. In effect, part of the senior executives' function at Gati is to help employees understand the strategic significance or potential of their ideas and actions.

On a granular level, a special team at the head office handles decisions related to organization-wide issues. Toward this end, a cross-functional meeting occurs twice a week. A similar body is in place at the zonal level. This group is empowered to make their own operational decisions, whereas broader issues are handled by the head office. The committee at the head office and the zones has similar composition. The group includes heads of respective functions: accounts, HR, facilities, and business. Each one has a chairman who is appointed quarterly. Zonal issues are discussed and decisions are made. Once this is done, the plans are implemented.

An interesting feature of this setup is the provision of "escalations." Decisions outside the purview of the zones, such as those relating to policy matters, are sent up for intervention by the home office. Also, if a zone is unable to arrive at a consensus, they escalate the matter to the head office for conflict resolution. Further, when a zone is affected by a decision made at a higher level, it can approach the head office with their concerns about the matter.

As managing director, Agarwal has visited each and every branch of Gati, and says that is oftentimes where strategy ideas come from. "I do a lot of travelling around the country. I get to meet a lot of people in the lower hierarchy of the organization, and sometimes even a stray remark from them helps us pick up the threats. Then I share this with the senior team and we try to process them," he says.[18] These excursions have helped Agarwal grasp the state of affairs in every nook and cranny of the country.

This system of bottom-up planning with top-down supervision continues to work for Gati. India's leader in express distribution and supply chain solutions, Gati has grown to become a $213 million company today,[19] even taking into account the 50 percent devaluation of the rupee in 2013.

Yet, success aside, are Gati's lessons widely applicable? The bottom-up process is a solid fit with Gati's culture and structure. An entrepreneur, Agarwal envisioned a company with few layers. It is in a logistically complex industry, yet the risks are fairly predictable. But is it realistic to expect a bottom-up approach to decisions and planning, which expands the number of people involved in the process, to work within an organization operating in a sector with higher levels of chaos and uncertainty?

Consider a sprawling sector such as oil and gas. Most major oil companies have a top-down management structure. It is a highly chaotic business where even one misstep can have global repercussions that roil the financial markets. These companies contend with global warming, regulatory issues, geopolitical unrest, price wars, and much, much more. Therefore, the stakes are high and control is very tight.

Take ExxonMobil, for example. The company is a poster child for standardized processes and quantitative performance measurement tools such as Six Sigma. They minimize deviation and maximize control. Yet, oil is a commodity, subject to the laws of supply and demand, not to mention wild price swings stemming from any number of factors outside their control. With that in mind, ExxonMobil has certain contingencies in place to address their broad spectrum of risks. They engage in across-the-board scenario planning, first and foremost, and country-specific financial modeling, to name just two. But this is not enough to make it feasible for ExxonMobil to take its chances in the most chaotic markets in the world, including parts of Africa and Central America. Even following acquisition and alliances, they have continued to exit these oil-rich markets because conditions on the ground change too fast. That much chaos and complexity is not compatible with ExxonMobil's centralized planning approach and standardized processes. They leave these markets to others—chiefly Total S.A.

A French multinational and one of the largest oil companies in the world, Total covers the entire oil and gas value chain, from crude oil and natural gas exploration and production to international oil and product trading. Even with their impressive scale, what is most interesting about Total is their capability to operate in the most turbulent markets in the world—they thrive amid chaos. In fact, when ExxonMobil exited several of their businesses in Africa in 2006, Total stepped in to buy their assets in order to deepen their own interest in the oil rich region. At the time, they agreed to buy ExxonMobil's fuels and lubricants businesses in fourteen African countries. The purchase included about five hundred service stations and twenty-nine terminals and depots.[20] The transaction pushed Total's share of Africa's fuel marketing to 10.8 percent, surpassing Royal Dutch Shell as the largest seller of gasoline, diesel, and other products in the region.

What makes Total different from ExxonMobil and BP? They give their managers considerably more latitude in how they operate. Their approach is different from Gati's in that the actual strategy of the organization remains fairly top-down and uniform across the organization, but it is how they *implement* the strategy that changes from country to country.

How do they make this work? Total's processes are mostly informal, and they engage and empower regional country managers to steer their strategy. These country managers are mostly French, so Total can call them their own; yet, they are immersed in the culture of their respective areas. Not only does each country manager have deep country-specific expertise but they also have a high degree of freedom and authority. This allows them to act quickly to respond to conditions as they arise on the ground. These country managers—fully enabled to act—are the glue that holds Total's approach together.

For Total, oil exploration and production are the main lines of activity. Therefore, in a world where new resources have to be prospected and delivered in the face of highly challenging circumstances, a high level of regional expertise is their chief competitive advantage. As the demand for oil and gas continues to grow due to pressure from emerging economies, Total's process has yielded large discoveries of oil in places like Bolivia, French Guiana, and Azerbaijan.[21] In 2013, Total started an operation at Kashagan with North Caspian Operating Company to harvest the largest discovery of oil reserves since 1968.[22]

Expanding the number of people who are empowered to act independently is a crucial part of the decentralized management structure at Total. They have a formal strategy, but the process for execution is flexible and informal. This flexibility enables the organization to adapt to a changing external environment. Strategy as a bottom-up phenomenon is a second-order effect of their informal processes, allowing more individuals within the organization the freedom to adapt and learn. And they use what they learn to adjust their strategy to suit current conditions. This flexibility helps Total operate in turbulent markets where conditions change fast.

Making Bottom-Up Strategy Stick

A bottom-up approach to strategy works for Total because country managers are essentially running their own businesses—they have the latitude to respond and adapt to conditions on the ground. The majlis system in Dubai, described in chapter 2, is a different model altogether, and yet it enables bottom-up strategy creation as well. As we saw, majlis is an Arab tradition designed to enable the free flow of ideas up and down a chain of command. Leaders in Dubai use majlis to make their values and priorities widely known. But majlis can also be used to crowdsource solutions and test ideas on people all across an organization.

When was the last time you heard a CEO present a new strategy and finish like this: "Now tell me everything you think is wrong with this. Help me poke holes in it." This seldom occurs in the West because designing strategy is considered to be a reflection of a CEO's intellect, and it becomes a measure of his or her success. Thus, a challenge to strategic direction is taken as a personal affront. Yet in many rapidly changing environments around the world the exact opposite occurs. In Dubai, for example, this type of sentiment is common: "We know this strategy is about 90 percent correct, now let's share it within the company and get some feedback." They know from experience that getting a strategy right on their own will take twice as long—and the market will have moved on. It is built into their process to get input from the employees who are closest to frontline customers. In this case, they use the majlis to establish a dialogue with the people who are most likely to have the latest intelligence.

Like launching a beta version in software or the soft release of a product, this one-to-many interaction enables not only feedback from stakeholders and the market but also iteration before a strategy is considered a done deal. Strategic planning of this type combines a bottom-up and top-down approach. It should be noted that under these conditions the role of senior managers is fundamentally altered—their job is no longer to *initiate* innovation (by developing every new strategy on their own) but to *endorse* innovation (by putting resources behind other people's ideas and scaling them up across the entire organization).

Having seen this expansion tool in action, a bottom-up approach works best when certain principles are put into play:

1. Combine the formal and informal. Strategy creation can become a formal, invitation-only dance that is rife with pomp and circumstance. One of the reasons the majlis system works so well is because it has a degree of informality. Employees with a good idea know they can step up and have their say. Different people attend each gathering and the exchange is brief and off the cuff. The formal "task force" approach that is common in the West has its limitations; it is vulnerable to high-level lobbying and is frequently marred by analysis paralysis. The formality can slow the process down. At Majlis, individuals express what is on their mind—ideas, concerns, and solutions—and the leader usually makes a decision immediately. They can then move on to what is next without lengthy debate. By opening up the conversation to many more people, Majlis makes strategy creation a collective endeavor that is also fast and efficient.

Codifying informal interactions by integrating them into the strategy process creates a dynamic where a multitude of ideas are captured from across the organization and decisions are made more quickly. This is one of the primary innovations of the Strategic Shock Absorbers—they build a bridge between formal and formal interactions, smoothing out the strengths and weaknesses of each, to make planning faster and more effective.

India's largest commercial real estate developer, DLF, combines formal/top-down and informal/bottom-up planning in this way. In a discussion about how to make that work, Saurabh Chawla, senior vice president of finance, said: "We can have thousands of acres of land but unless we have people who believe that they can monetize it into cash, it's useless for us." He went on to say that there can't be any disconnect between the strategic vision, the strategic plan, and the actual operating plan.[23]

To put that idea into play, DLF's top-down approach to strategic planning is complemented by an equal measure of participation from middle managers. Every business unit presents its own plans for the coming six months. These plans and projections—containing balance sheets, profit and loss statements, and cash flow results—are typically reviewed by the top management to ensure that they mesh with the company's interests. The dual approach is visible throughout the various planning horizons at DLF. Planning is then fine-tuned based on external inputs such as global events. What is derived from customers and suppliers is also incorporated. This manner of integrating formal and informal planning brings more people into the process, while allowing management to maintain a level of control.

2. Don't punish the messenger. The majlis model is an example of an environment where people can speak truth to power and authority. Assuming they are well intentioned and have their facts straight, it is appropriate for people to address even the Sheikh himself. It's built into the culture of the majlis. Recall the story of the shopkeeper who brought his problem to the Sheikh. *"My shop is being blocked by traffic from a construction site."* That was a courageous moment for the shopkeeper and he was rewarded. The Sheikh solved his problem on the spot and earned a loyal subject in the process.

Bottom-up strategy creation gets more people involved, thereby generating buy-in. One moment like that in a Western organization can turn the tide. You have earned a loyal employee for life while simultaneously enhancing your reputation. Yet, if people get punished for poking holes in the strategy, the opposite occurs. Executives need to have the courage to listen and be humble. After all, who are the employees most likely to notice potential problems with strategy? Your best and brightest. Ignore them and the company loses its most valuable asset—talent. Can the people in your organization step up and express their ideas and concerns without fear of fallout or retribution?

3. Be a good listener. Making bottom-up planning fruitful requires a shift in mind-set. Leaders need to listen for ideas and intelligence and be in a position to act on them. In the case of Welspun Limited, one of the largest terry cloth towel makers in the world, one idea from the sales team dramatically expanded their business. As one of the few companies, like Arvind Mills, remaining from the formerly glorious textile mills of Mumbai, Welspun stands in the shadow of the mighty fallen textile giants of yesteryear. They might have suffered a similar fate to so many others had it not been for the foresight of two gentlemen—B. K. Goenka and Rajesh R. Mandawe-wala, the company's joint managing directors. These directors' capacity to take calculated risks and effect timely moves has been instrumental in Welspun's success. In terms of strategic planning, the pair and their wider team value on-the-ground experience above pure analytics and professional management, and it is something they consider to be an ingredient of their long-term success.

"We are good listeners," remarks M. L. Mittal, former executive director of finance at Welspun India Ltd.[24] "When we make decisions, we give more weight to the operating team. We don't [rely exclusively on] statistics prepared by young MBAs without any practical experience."[25] He went on to say that they consistently turn to managers in the field to inform not only their projections and product development but also their long-range planning; "they are in the business day in and day out. They would know better than anyone sitting behind closed doors," Mittal says.[26]

In 2004, for example, upon the advice of a sales manager, Welspun went from producing and selling mostly towels to dis-tributing a much larger product line including sheets and rugs. When the idea came in from the field, management picked it up, and it was the basis of a major expansion.

Just as they welcome intelligence, Welspun also makes data readily available to individuals throughout the organization. If all employees are potential decision makers and strategists, then they need access to updated data to ensure that fast decisions are informed by key information. According to Uttam Newalkar, "Information is shared by everybody. If [a Towel Marketing Executive] is travelling abroad and needs to quote prices for towels, then he needs to know the price of yarn."[27] It is a sort of virtuous circle. The flow of data to line managers informs their thinking, and they send market data back up to management to inform projections and strategic planning.

4. Consider the culture. The biggest challenge to bottom-up strategy creation is cultural. It is difficult for senior executives in some corporate cultures to understand that their jobs rest on the strategic ideas of others. Today's global workforce is arguably the best trained in history. People won't sit back and allow others (even a CEO) to take credit for their ideas. Conversely, credit a strategy idea to one of your customer service reps, and the story becomes part of the corporate culture. There is huge power and ongoing payback in bringing more people into the process.

This type of payback is evident at companies such as Zappos, where individuals across the organization are fully plugged in to what is happening in the market. People working on the call center at Zappos take pride in that fact that the intelligence they collect is fully utilized. As a result, turnover is extremely low. Zappos has so many job applicants for their call center that they turn away 90 percent of the people who apply. Their acceptance rate rivals that of Harvard University.[28] Why? People's ideas are taken seriously and they are a part of the strategy process.

In order to make bottom-up strategy effective, there needs to be understanding across the company about the wider goals and values. Starting from a common place saves time and brings people together. Getting on the same page is something that executives at Arvind Mills told me they work hard at. Everyone, from the finance teams to the weavers and loomers, understands that Arvind is not a "fashion guru" and it does not take extreme steps such as using artificial neural networks to predict fashion trends.[29] Their main goal is try to stay close to the customer's point of view and everyone works with that in mind.

Creating a means for bottom-up strategy speeds communication flow and creates a self-reinforcing loop. As we saw with Mahindra & Mahindra, a bottom-up approach can create a true competitive advantage. If your business is all about consistency—as in ExxonMobil—then the traditional top-down mode, with best practices and a Six Sigma approach, is appropriate. Yet, in a world of change and unpredictability, where agility and adaptation allow organizations to meet market needs, strategic planning needs to be a collective endeavor. Misalignment occurs at the fringes—a salesperson who is dealing with the difficult client or a manager who connects with suppliers—and not exclusively in the center. Given the fast pace of change, the moment is right for this type of reverse innovation of the strategic planning processes to be built in to existing formal structures.

The Art of Management: Agility

The tools above come together in the Agility shock absorber to deliver speed and flexibility. As part of constant adaptation, *frequent planning* is a compression mode, compressing time to make strategic planning fast and ongoing as opposed to episodic. Zara, Mahindra & Mahindra, and Charles & Keith all plan faster and more frequently using market intelligence that flows into the organization. The *corporate concierge* is a compression tool that essentially delivers the same benefit. Information flows in through one well-informed point of entry and is curated and funneled to the appropriate places in the company. In this case, compressing the gatekeeper function with an ambassador role means valuable information is captured, assessed, and distributed for faster planning and decisions.

Bottom-up strategy is an expansion tool. In this case it calls for empowering many more people to get involved in strategy creation and it opens up new options. Total, DLF, and Gati each made a point in this way of making strategy creation a collective endeavor. As in the majlis, casting a wider net for ideas means that the market plays a larger part in informing strategy moves. At the same time, bottom-up strategy also delivers loyalty and engagement internally.

These tools, like the others in this book, are ongoing modes of operating. They flow together and require judgment to determine where on a spectrum they can and should be put into practice. The art of management involves knowing when to oscillate between compression and expansion and between the different shock absorbers presented in this book. This is dictated by the market environment and industry conditions. Like shock absorbers in a car, these tools will help absorb bumps and surprises before they destabilize operations. The ideal is that, in time, the mechanics of the shock absorbers will become almost second nature.

As with every fresh tool at our disposal, using the Agility shock absorber entails trial and error. In today's environment the surprises are ongoing and one bump leads right into another. As part of that reality, one of the things shock absorbers enable is constant learning. When you choose to compress time or information, or expand resources and options—or any combination of these variables—you can ask yourself: *what have I learned?* You will notice that many of the strategy modes in the Agility shock absorber are all about this type of learning. What can the market tell me? (Constant adaptation.) What can my employees tell me? (Bottom-up strategy.) When you learn something new it may indicate a time to expand (bottom-up strategy) as opposed to compress (corporate concierge), or vice versa. The shock absorbers also identify cycles. In some instances, reacting to turbulence will require compression first and then expansion. At other times the opposite will be true.

The art of management involves knowing how long to remain in a certain mode. Wait too long to change and you are inefficient; move on too quickly to the next mode and you are minimizing learning. The key in the Agility shock absorber, as in the others, is using what you learn to adapt, fast and flexibly, as situations and conditions change. Every time you learn something new it will provide a better understanding of the situation for the next time around.

4

Momentum

Speeding Past Shocks
and Surprises

The Finnish communications giant Nokia dominated the market for tiny and trendy mobile phones in 2006. They essentially invented the category in the late 1990s, and quickly became the most valued brand in Europe. Obsessive about connecting with customers, Nokia relied on user-generated innovation to steer the ship. They never made a move without testing it first with consumers. Then, six short months later, Apple introduced the iPhone. It was a stunning surprise. The first in a long line of smartphones, Apple (and later Samsung) backed Nokia into a corner from which they will most likely never fully emerge.

Netflix, conversely, was on the winning side of surprise in 2009–10, when their disruptive business model pushed their leading competitor, Blockbuster, into Chapter 11.[1] With a low-cost structure and an innovator's edge, Netflix offered customers convenience and a price advantage at a time when Blockbuster was overexposed on the retail side. For their part, Netflix mined a mountain of big data, using analytics to decide tactical maneuvers. And yet, even Netflix was caught off guard in 2012, when their own pricing strategy backfired, choking profits for three consecutive quarters and causing customer churn to skyrocket. The surprise left them reeling in the short term.[2]

Despite their respective market positions and steady reliance on intelligence, both companies encountered surprises that they could not readily absorb, and they lost their momentum in the market. Bumps in the terrain are unavoidable. In the same way that even a careful driver invariably encounters potholes, companies run up against unexpected events. No matter how ardently an organization tries to anticipate them, surprises—from global economic turmoil to unforeseen upstart competitors—occur. What is of vital importance, however, is developing the capability to absorb shocks and maintain momentum without destabilizing the entire company.

Based on my research into how the best global companies succeed in fast-changing environments, I have seen that companies absorb shocks and retain their momentum when

Figure 4.1 The Momentum Shock Absorber

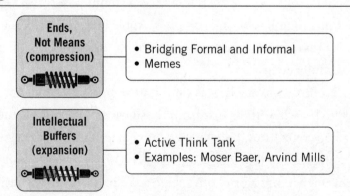

- Ends, Not Means (compression)
  - Bridging Formal and Informal
  - Memes
- Intellectual Buffers (expansion)
  - Active Think Tank
  - Examples: Moser Baer, Arvind Mills

they have two elements in place. First, they *focus on the end versus the means*; and, second, they *create intellectual buffers*. As we will see, these two ideas have something significant in common. As part of the Strategic Shock Absorbers, they come together as a bridge to integrate the formal and informal elements of strategy.

Mastering the End Versus Means

Imagine yourself at a traffic intersection trying to make your way across the street on foot. Crossing the street looks different depending on where you are in the world. In the United States and much of Continental Europe, there are clearly marked crosswalks with signals and auditory cues. Pedestrians have the right of way and vehicles must yield. In England there are zebra crossings: space demarcated by lines on the road with flashing orange lights at either side. When a pedestrian puts a foot into the crosswalk it is as if he or she has become divinely empowered, like Moses parting the Red Sea. This picture stands in stark contrast with a pedestrian trying to cross the road in India. First, there are seldom crosswalks in India. And it would not matter if there were, because no one yields to pedestrians. In China it is even more dangerous. They have crosswalks and pedestrian signals, similar to the West, but people drive like they are in India—no one yields to pedestrians. Like many Westerners, I learned this one the hard way.

In the United States and Europe, then, it is fairly simple to explain to someone how to cross the street. There is one standard, predictable, and simple procedure. Compare that to

India, where there is no single optimal procedure that can be explained in advance. Instead, crossing the road in India entails reacting quickly to conditions on the ground at any given moment. One time you may inch forward, sprint back, leap over a cow, and crawl under a camel to get across. The next time you traverse the same road something entirely different may be what gets you across unharmed. There is no way to know in advance—no way to accurately predict what strategy will work.

Now let's put this analogy into a business context. In a world built around Six Sigma and disciplined performance management tools, most businesses embrace one optimal way to perform activities. It becomes the centerpiece around which they operate. A standard process defines how contracts are approved, services are priced, goods are manufactured, and orders are shipped. People are hired, trained, and tested based on preestablished standards. In such an environment, where there is one predictable, right way to do everything, it seems only logical to evaluate people's performance according to how well they achieve interim goals. These interim goals, after all, are considered critical stepping stones along the crosswalk to achieving results.

Yet, this mode creates a potentially dangerous trap. Operating an enterprise today is like crossing the road in India. The pace of change requires latitude and agility. When markets and competitors are shifting and changing frequently there is no *one best way* to succeed—no one standard and predictable tactical approach. An overreliance on standardized strategic targets causes people to take their eyes away from the big picture to focus on interim milestones. Companies are slow to see shifts in their environment when they are dedicated to measuring interim performance objectives. Even worse, they fail to recognize when the overall strategic objective itself has shifted.

Like the pedestrian in India, companies need to be in a position to change direction—leaping over a cow and crawling under a camel or two. Achieving results in a permanently turbulent environment requires a focus on the end goal—and watching to see if it has shifted—as opposed to institutionalizing the one best way to get there.

Focusing on the ends, not the means, is a compression capability that is common within the technology space. It is about homing in on the result or objective that is most critical to success and toeing the line there, because everything else may change as the environment shifts. Let's take Google as an example. With their larger goal being to *access and control as much critical information as possible*, Google has gone on to create product after new product. From Gmail and Google Maps to Google Earth to Android, every diverse move they have made has been designed to reach that one end—collect more data. The Googles and Apples of the world can't afford to lose sight of their broad primary objectives. After all, their competitive environment and underlying business assumptions are shifting constantly and fundamentally—so they could very well be in one business in January and a different business altogether by June. The underlying business model in Google's space is designed for change even as their overarching goal has remained constant.

When everything else is changing, that overarching end goal, along with an organization's core values, remains the guiding light. Fast change is a contagion that has spread well beyond the technology space across *all companies everywhere.* As we have seen, this is certainly the case in countries such as India, where even the largest organizations, no matter their sector or size, have needed to learn to operate in a mode of constant turbulence in order to succeed. Take big retail as a case in point.

An enduring image that confronts foreigners in India is its loud, crowded bazaars, stacked high with exotic foods and wares spilling over into the streets. Even now, most everyday purchases there are the outcome of hard bargaining between the unrelenting street vendor and an ever-suspicious buyer. Any comparisons to shopping at a Walmart store in the United States immediately evoke the stark contrast between retail in India vis-à-vis its Western counterparts.

Kishore Biyani, CEO of Future Group, grasped the importance of this difference early on.[3] Now an immensely well-known figure in Indian industry, Biyani was first to break ground and usher large-scale organized retail—trading activities undertaken by licensed retailers registered for sales tax, income tax, and so on—into India. Yet, he did so shrewdly and with a decidedly local flavor.

In 2001, Future Group's flagship, the umbrella company Pantaloon Retail, launched its popular low-cost "hypermarket" retailer: Big Bazaar. Aimed at providing a local marketplace feel, Big Bazaar is the largest hypermarket chain of its kind. As of spring 2012 there were 162 stores across 95 cities and towns in India covering around 16 million square feet of retail space and serving around 300 million customers each year.[4] Designed as an agglomeration of Indian markets, Big Bazaar features clusters offering a wide range of merchandise including apparel, food products, books, furniture, and electronics.

The retail chain has served as the backbone of Future Group in several ways. For one, the success of Big Bazaar over time has strengthened Future Group financially. Their performance has been impressive compared to other players in the market. In addition, their innovation in terms of strategic planning and performance management has set the standard for the wider organization. Yet, perhaps Big Bazaar's most notable contribution to Future Group has been its role as a bellwether. Because they sell such a wide range of consumer goods, the store serves as an intelligence unit. They are a looking glass into the mind of the Indian consumer. What Future Group learns from Big Bazaar informs how they stock and merchandise their other businesses.

Launched at a time marked by incredible economic and cultural transformation all across India, Big Bazaar and other Future Group businesses have managed to meet the needs of a shifting marketplace, absorbing bumps and retaining momentum, in large part by focusing squarely on their end goals, as opposed to the means by which they achieve success. This plays out in terms of strategy planning in a number of ways that show how Future Group integrates formal and informal processes. As illustrated in the following section, they use formal planning tools to communicate and carefully manage their nonnegotiable primary goals, and informal planning to empower individuals throughout the company to achieve those goals in ways they see fit. Focusing on the ends versus the means is a compression tool that nonetheless offers a range of freedom for managers throughout an organization.

Formal Planning

The *formal* strategic planning process at Future Group consists of two main components: Business Plans and Annual Budgeting. Both components have different planning horizons and varying degrees of formality. In addition, they have differentiated involvement from four main levels of management—managing director, board of directors, CEOs, and middle and junior management.

Business plans. Business Plans at Future Group are an instrument for high-level strategy. They are focused on achieving goals with a planning horizon of three years. These are financial goals that, very broadly, include bottom- and top-line targets and return-on-capital employed (ROCE), among others. The business plan does not specify the steps to be taken to achieve targets but only provides yearly benchmarks for review. These targets, once set, are not ever revised or altered. In order to achieve targets, the company maps out a course of action that is fully alterable. Business plan targets are immovable, but the ways to achieve them change according to market conditions and other externalities.

Annual budgeting. Annual budgeting is the third and final more formal planning tool employed at Future Group. This exercise deals primarily with making budgetary allocations for the coming year. Budgets not only delineate the amount of funds to be used for completing targets but also specify the amounts to be expended on salaries, support functions, and the like. Budgets also make special provisions for eventualities and exceptional circumstances. The annual budgeting exercise involves the managing director, CFO of Future Group, as well as the board of directors of the company. Budgets are made in the beginning of the every financial year and allocations to all initiatives are decided in advance. Modes of availing allocated provisions are also specified. Overall, this exercise seeks to avoid any financial bottlenecks and excesses that might occur while undertaking and executing the various targets. In a way, annual budgeting attaches monetary value to and assesses the cost of executing new initiatives.

These formal planning processes are generally executed with precision at Future Group to establish and manage their major end goals, but they are routine until you factor in their interplay with a number of informal ways of working that enable them to move quickly to seize opportunities and respond to surprise events.

Informal Practices

Informal strategy planning, with less oversight and structure, is the other primary piece of the company's efforts to manage to the end result as opposed to micromanaging the means. Borne of insights accumulated over several years, this is what enables Future Group to hedge risks inherent in the retail sector and the Indian marketplace. For instance, it helps them manage surprises pertaining to government policy uncertainty, rolling out new and untested retail formats, and competing for quality human resources in a fast-growing market. In a number of ways, the informal planning here is as crucial to success as the more formal processes.

Ideas are formed on the ground. Designed as laboratories of ideation, most of Future Group's new retail concepts are conceived and tested at the local level. In effect, the footfalls on the ground provide a sample for gauging the pulse of consumers. In this regard, the twin foci at Future Group are in developing fresh retail formats and determining the specific product mix.

According to Sanjeev Agrawal, CEO of Pantaloons, the success of Big Bazaar and other Future Group brands is linked to the emotional connection between the consumer and the stores.[5] Future Group considers its ability to devise entirely new businesses and test their feasibility on the ground to be a key asset. Apart from its established retail formats—including Pantaloons and Big Bazaar—Future Group generally has several new retail ideas at various stages of development. The thinking is that retail is a business that requires constant updates in order to remain current and so keeping an ear close to the ground to recognize trends should make up the cornerstones of the group's strategy. From a ten-thousand-foot perspective, this is how they focus on the end result and vary the means in response to changing conditions.

According to Agrawal: "Every store has to reflect the ethos of the city or locality it is a part of. Therefore, efforts aimed at understanding consumers are qualitative and not driven much by numbers."[6] Instead, businesses are built and refined based on observing consumer behavior.

The concept of Big Bazaar, for example, came out of an informal study undertaken by Kishor Biyani and his team back in 2001.[7] Using the Indian city of Hyderabad as its nodal center, the study examined retail stores in the southern region of India. Most of the observations from the study veered heavily toward purely subjective insights rather than quantitative detail. The running of stores was not the main focus of the effort—the emphasis was on learning how Indians shopped.

A combination of monitoring local consumption habits and studying each market prior to launch are the utterly simple main ingredients for Future Group's strategy for market entry. Yet, this is not the only way the organization proceeds. Damodar Mall, CEO of the Incubation & Innovation division, which is responsible for the evolution and establishment of new ventures, is quick to point out that all manner of other conventional research—market sizing, target population, retail locations, ethnographic study, and so on—is also a part of the planning process.[8] However, this is never where ideas are formed; rather, this is where they are verified.

An additional positive byproduct of the continuous rollout of new ventures at Future Group is a "learning from mistakes" philosophy. Mall claims that when a team has ideas for a new retail format or product, the focus is on crystallizing ideas and launching prototypes in key markets.[9] They do not seek to articulate a fixed business plan with estimates and forecasts before launch. Though the basic parameters of success and failure of new ideas are written down, not much by way of energy or resources are allocated to "predicting the future." Instead, the team takes feedback straight from the consumers by noting their reactions to prototypes. On the question of the cost attached to mistakes, Mall says that the value of the learning derived from the prototypes and its further application in other ventures offsets any financial spillage.

Even closer to the ground than new businesses, the actual product mix at Big Bazaar varies from store to store. According to Damodar, only 70 percent of the product mix is uniform across the nation, while the remaining 30 percent is developed on the basis of specific consumer demand.[10] The 30 percent is decided on the shop floor by observing customers and understanding their specific needs. Often, these insights are developed by the store staff and then passed up the ladder to executives.

One example of tailoring the product mix at Future Group to serve local needs was the decision to sell the burqa—the veil worn by Muslim women. Pantaloon's store in central Mumbai was the first of its type to sell burqas. The idea was prompted by the observation that a sizable segment of the local consumers was made up of Muslim women. This observation was later refined into a product line after further study revealed that varying styles and designs were preferred by women in different Muslim communities. The decision to sell burqas was made based on anecdotal evidence; however, the design and styles of the larger product line was determined through research. This combination of formal and informal processes allows for greater flexibility in regard to how the company achieves long-term end goals.

Using Memes as a Means to an End

As part of their strategy planning, Future Group uses memes in several different ways both externally and internally. When we think of memes, most of us think about what popular ideas are making the rounds out in the world. Memes can oftentimes be identified by what is trending online—for example, "soccer moms" in the mid-1990s or "tiger moms" more recently.

At Future Group, they set up a "Center for Memetics." The primary task of the center is to identify memes that influence target groups of consumers. In part, the center uses these memes as the basis for new product ideas. For example, the center floats concepts such as creating "a TV that goes mute when you receive a phone call" or "in-the-aisle billing and payment options at hypermarkets."

Beyond specific innovations, Future Group uses the center to analyze the wider context of their environment and understand the customer in a changing society. This broader use of market intelligence is a little different from the norm. For example, when Nokia used customer research in the early 1990s (as they do today), they mined it to identify incremental improvements for their products. Future Group also uses it to capture the broad themes (such as time saving and multitasking) affecting Indian consumers, and builds them into their retail concepts and product mix.

This wide-lens approach to market research combines a subjective grasp of consumer behavior with verifiable data. The mix enables organizations to fix their focus on end results without defining one specific tactical approach. However, the methodology hinges on the experience of employees. In part, this brings to light the crucial role of human resources. Retention of the right talent at the top, and building a team of handpicked executives, are a priority.

Internally, Future Group uses memes to convey its overall vision to its thirty-five thousand employees.[11] Building on memes, Pantaloon Retail uses stories to inculcate employees into its fold. Values are communicated through stories that illustrate, for example, why creativity is considered a key element of working at Pantaloon Retail, or how a sense of responsibility is encouraged in each employee, and so on. These memes are built into regular training sessions for junior and middle-level management and employees. They are also used as a primary tool for internal communication. Formally and informally, memes can produce parity in understanding end goals and values for employees, and reinforce the sense of working creatively toward one common goal.

Executives as entrepreneurs. Devising and rapidly prototyping new retail formats frequently can be risky. One way to instill a sense of responsibility among employees is to entrust them with executing new businesses as an entrepreneur would. Future Group achieves this, in part, by mitigating the risk exposure to each individual. For example, the parameters for assessing so-called surrogate entrepreneurs working on a new initiative are different from those used to assess the business heads of established ventures. Proven business models, on the one hand, have to deliver on aspects such as speed of scale-up, uniformity of operating discipline, improvements in the bottom lines, and the like. On the other hand, for new initiatives, gaining customer insights, getting the design right, prototyping, and proving the business model is all accorded a higher priority than efficiencies. By classifying business ventures into either proven or new initiatives, the group is able to provide an encouraging environment for new business ideas, insulating them somewhat from pressures of managing for the bottom line.

Another angle to surrogate entrepreneurship is by making the job roles of senior managers more flexible and fluid. Most business heads at Future Group operate in defined functional areas; however, they are also expected to share knowledge and offer opinions on matters outside their own domain. This diffuses the chance of developing a myopic view of their respective responsibilities. They are also expected to have a complete view of the group's businesses and participate in developing a wide range of new ventures. In principle, this flexibility and independence results in a multilateral approach to decision making. Importantly, it also allows individuals to make the "final call" in matters of execution.

Beyond senior executives, the entrepreneurial mode requires a culture of empowerment across an organization. At Future Group, for instance, store managers make the call about the placement of products, shelf space, and customer service. For example, Gurpreet Singh Bhatia, general manager of a Big Bazaar in Mumbai, says that his insights on consumer likes and dislikes are incorporated into decision making. He is cleared in advance to make decisions about inventory and shelf space in his store.[12] He is apprised of the organization's overall objectives and works creatively and somewhat independently to achieve them.

Formulating strategy with a focus on end results stems from the interplay between formal planning and informal processes. Using tools from the Strategic Shock Absorbers, Future Group manages to integrate both modes. Formal processes—annual budgeting and business plans—were adopted and cemented during the early years. They are the mandatory practices that establish the targets for the company and its managers. Informal processes are the soft lessons learned over years of experimentation. They are the best practices and guidelines that can be modified and adapted as conditions on the ground change.

Future Group also uses the balanced scorecard (BSC). This is important because, like the Strategic Shock Absorbers, BSC uses formal and informal inputs. Future Group's balanced scorecard amounts to detailed lists of annual targets composed of four main elements: financials, customer targets, internal process, and learning and growth targets. These are very specific tasks, each of which is assigned to a concept owner. BSC is a critical tool at Future Group because it brings quantitative and nonquantitative elements together in one place. The concept owners act as the balancing mechanism—championing innovative ideas within the structure of the scorecards. They are given timelines that specify completion within one year. These timelines are a part of the scorecards and are synchronized with each other in case the accomplishment of some tasks should act as enablers for some others.

What BSC and the Strategic Shock Absorbers illustrate is that both formal and informal mechanisms are necessary. In the case of the shock absorbers, they are geared specifically to allow companies to respond quickly to surprise bumps and opportunities and still maintain operating momentum.

A central rationale for mastering the art of the informal, as well as formal, elements of strategy is similar to what we in the West think about as balancing left- and right-brain approaches. Until recently, Western companies have been able to focus heavily on the formal side—by relying on solid execution. However, as markets have become fully global, with change and turbulence disrupting every industry, we see that flawless execution is necessary but not nearly sufficient. The

Figure 4.2 Perceived Importance of Different Levels of Management in the Strategic Planning Process (in Percent)

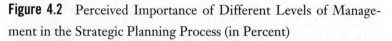

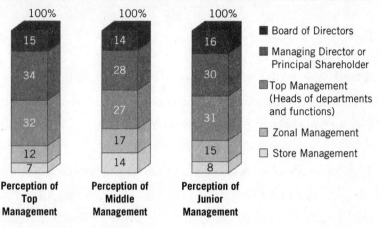

Source: Internal Opinion Survey.

Figure 4.3 Perceived Importance of Formal and Informal Communication in the Strategic Planning Process (in Percent)

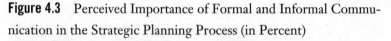

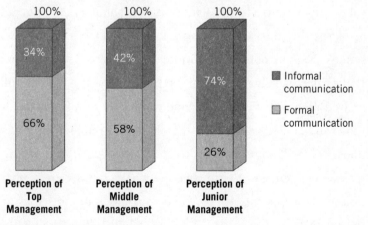

Source: Internal Opinion Survey.

need to bridge formal and informal strategy has become a vital part of the new paradigm for success. This idea will come up again and again, including in our discussion of Intellectual Buffers later in this chapter.

The Upside of Ends Versus Means

Focusing on ends over means has a few notable benefits that I've seen play out at companies I've researched.

1. Results above process. Companies can get bogged down adhering to strict structure and they lose sight of what really matters. Dabur Limited, for example, a hundred-year-old "Ayurvedics" manufacturer based on a thousand-year-old science, uses their emphasis on ends over means to target what matters most to them—keeping their business current.

Ayurvedics is a medicinal system native to the Indian subcontinent and a form of alternative medicine that is literally as old as the hills. Once upon a time, the Dabur[13] name was synonymous in consumers' minds with the old banyan tree. It produced lively medicinal brands across several carefully crafted niches. It became a name to reckon with in the health tonic and oral-care powder segments. Entrenched in Indian households, Dabur's ability to deliver results faced its first serious challenge with the massive change and development in India during the 1990s. This turbulent decade sounded the death knell for many well-established Indian brands, but Dabur matched the changing times by changing itself faster. In large part, the organization adopted an unwavering focus on ends over means.

According to Jude Magima, head of supply chain for Dabur India, their model of decision making, critically dependent on achieving results, is exactly the emphasis that separates Dabur from many companies in the United States and Europe. Western companies, he said, plan and execute with an eye on a process, rather than on achieving objectives.[14]

As a family-owned business, establishing an emphasis on results over process was critical for keeping Dabur out of the weeds and moving forward. With that in mind, they establish and formally agree upon clear and measurable goals and then they track them rigorously. If these goals are seen to be "out of grasp" at any time during the execution phase, the management committee is asked to find a suitable course correction. In addition, the committee not only tracks results, but it also tracks changes in the marketplace that may affect the feasibility of strategic vision itself.

Rajan explains: "How good are you at determining what the other players are about to do? In India, this is critical. Success lies in your ability to react to that change very quickly to gain competitive advantage over the next person."

Today, with thinking that places results above process, Dabur has become one of India's largest consumer goods companies.

2. Ongoing/adaptive strategic planning. When results are prioritized above tactics, it is simpler to justify switching up the strategy to achieve objectives. With this, the strategy document itself, as well as the process, are not considered to be sacrosanct. Neither are interim quantitative benchmarks. As one executive at Indian denim manufacturer Arvind Mills told me: "[Above reaching quantitative benchmarks,] the more critical part is an assessment of where we are and where we are headed."[15] With that knowledge it is easier to decide how to get there.

3. *Establishes engagement.* Finally, an end-versus-means approach helps individuals remain engaged and anchored during organizational shifts. When everything else is in flux, clearly defined objectives give individuals a light in the distance. Furthermore, latitude in how one reaches objectives keeps employees engaged. RDS Bawa, the Group CFO at one of India's leading business news channels, told me: "From a strategic perspective, we have goals concerning where we want to be. We moved from being a content provider to being a telecaster, and from business news to general news. But in every venture, the single-point agenda has been to deliver news."[16] He said that precisely *how* they reach their overarching goal is reliant on the judgment of the individuals involved. Their clearly stated objective is what brings people together, while the freedom in execution mode keeps them engaged. The end takes prescience over the means.

Moving on to the second main tool in the Momentum shock absorber—Intellectual Buffers—the emphasis here is on creative ways to fortify companies during growth, change, or turbulence.

Intellectual Buffers, Not Physical Buffers

In the late 1970s and early 1980s, when the West was facing significant inflation for the first time in years, management scholars and practitioners turned to Japan for insights. One key observation they gleaned was that holding inventory and other forms of slack resources is bad for business in two ways. First, these "physical buffers" are expensive to hold. Not only do they require the initial financial investment, but additional warehousing costs and other expenses also come into play. Second, the excess inventory can cause a company to become disconnected from its external environment. They don't see that the world has changed because they must continue with the normal processes associated with distributing the accumulated inventory, much like a hibernating squirrel that has stored up nuts is insulated and cut off from a cold winter.

In response, management enacted just-in-time (JIT) and business process redesign (BPR), as well as the Lean Manu-facturing Movement beginning in the late 1980s and into the '90s. In the name of these new efficiencies, businesses eliminated excess inventory and other physical buffers including overhead and staff. The result of the JIT, BPR, and the Lean revolu-tions is that many companies have become like Formula 1 race cars—highly refined precision machines with not a bit of wasted space or extra weight. They have exactly what they need and nothing more. However, Formula 1 cars are only capable of high performance within a very limited range of conditions—that is, you do not take a Formula 1 car off road (at least not for very long) because it won't last on rough terrain. Similarly, many companies have taken out their "slack resources" just when they are facing some of the most unpredictable, challenging, and changing environments in recent history.

It is impossible to absorb the bumps and surprises that materialize without losing momentum when every last man, woman, and personal computer is already operating at full capacity. Cut to the bone, it can actually become more difficult to react quickly. How can companies run lean and still form fast and agile responses to bumps in the terrain? In my research I have found that the best way to manage this dilemma is by replacing traditional physical buffers—inventory and slack resources—with what I call intellectual buffers.

Intellectual buffers are ways that an organization can build up intangible advantages that lead to better decision making: management innovation, creative ideation, more effective communication, and smarter strategic thinking. This is achieved when companies can effectively leverage *people* at the same time that they bring better technology and communications to bear. Both ingredients are inextricably linked, but the people side of the equation is what tips the balance. This expansion tool counts on human capital to innovate in order to deliver on strategic objectives.

Intellectual buffers can be built up in several types, two of which I will describe here.

Active think tanks. A common type of intellectual buffer, active think tanks are a brain trust of functional specialists—people from both senior and junior ranks—who conduct a type of scenario planning. They meet regularly, often informally, to discuss what moves to make if various future events come to pass. More specifically, they consider implications and suggest responses to disruption before anything actually occurs. They look at resources to develop, markets to target, and they monitor the wider industry environment.

I place the emphasis on the "active" part of the think tank because the best of these are engaged, empowered, dynamic networks within an organization. I'm not talking about the tired task force or the annual ceremonial dinner where people come together simply to show their faces and make small talk. Active think tanks are a living, breathing mechanism for change.

With the passion of a stalker, Subir Mukherjee of Arvind Mills describes one of their active think tanks:

> We have fashion designers from different parts of the world. We have a consultant in the US who guides us on the American fashion trends in denim. Then, there is a Japanese designer; Japan is perceived to be the originator of any fashion. We have also involved one designer from Europe who is guiding us on the European side of things. For anybody, the market is mostly US or Europe—not for Arvind alone, but anybody. Most exports are also for conversion to garments and for final export to the US or Europe . . . Apart from the designers, we have our own team visiting the market, or we have our own offices as in the US . . . People are travelling on a continuous basis for presentations to the brands. Finally, we have our own design team here in Ahmedabad. Whatever information is picked from all the sources is synthesised into a product range by this team.[17]

Arvind Mills also utilizes a group of their own internal specialists in this way to consider new product development. In this case, they convene individuals from across their business—spinners, dyers, weavers, and specialists in finishing and washing—to discuss how Arvind might use the latest intelligence and technology to remain one step ahead. India's delivery service, Gati, has an active think tank with a similar makeup. Known as the SPG, the Strategy Planning Group recruits members not just from the executive committee but also from middle and junior management. It includes the heads of support functions like human resources, IT, accounts, and audit as well. Gati executive Rajeev Chopra says that the SPG is extremely broad based. "We pick [members] from functions all over the country and from different positions so that everybody gets a say," he says. Held twice a year, these sessions are for strategic planning and decision making.[18]

Active think tanks overlap and work in tandem with an organization's regular management team—which, in balance, may be too occupied driving the current strategy to speculate about future events and appropriate organizational responses. As a result of this type of intellectual buffer, when "surprise" events do materialize, a company is much quicker to respond because they have proposals and first-response scenarios at the ready.

Creating intellectual buffers is exactly how Moser Baer[19] was able to dominate in several different fields and reinvent itself many times over when they were in their prime, bypassing shocks and surprises that would have sidelined a less buffered organization.

The story begins in the 1980s with Moser Baer's CEO Deepak Puri. After completing his masters in mechanical engineering in London, Puri went on to start his business career in Kolkata, the capital of West Bengal. His first undertaking manufactured aluminum wires, pipes, and AC conductors. But before long, labor problems in the union hotbed of Kolkata forced him to shut down his facility. Undeterred, he started his second business, this time manufacturing recording devices for the banking industry. Again, before he could get settled, union members stormed in and poured acid on the machines. It was in the wake of those dramatic starts and stops that Puri launched Moser Baer in 1983. The organization went on to become the world's second largest manufacturer of blank digital media—CDs and DVDs. Shipping to over eighty-two countries, Moser Baer created a global footprint. They had state-of-the-art technology in their factories and Six Sigma manufacturing processes. Yet, all of this was not enough to remain competitive.

Their active think tank was formed when Moser Baer found itself up against several looming risks and uncertainties. First, their pricing power began deteriorating. Typically, products like CDs begin their life cycle at the upper end of the price scale. That was true in this case, particularly in the growth phase when CDs were considered an IT tool. But as applications grew, and computers themselves became entertainment centers, the variety of content that one could put on a CD led to their proliferation. Because of this, CDs today are treated like consumer packaged goods—they are sold quickly at a low cost. Therefore, following price and cost erosion, CDs have ended their journey as a commodity. As a result, companies like Moser Baer have neither pricing power nor control over the end-consumer market. The second significant risk was the potential for disruption. Products such as CDs and DVDs have a finite life. Competing technologies and new formats come along and upend the market, as was the case way back with audio cassettes and VHS tapes.

In the face of these immense challenges, Puri realized that he needed to bring on other strategic minds and professional managers to help plan for the future. Like most companies born in India, Moser Baer started as a family-driven enterprise. People at the time lived in multigenerational or extended family homes and the frequent dinner conversation was "How is business"? As companies grew, many kept the tradition of these mealtime business conversations, which, in the case of Moser Baer, evolved into the active think tank.

Professional management at Moser Baer led to changes in the leadership style. The organization moved from completely centralized decision making to becoming largely decentralized. In the process, a lot of the strategic ideas began to happen down the line, and day-to-day decisions were starting to be made by middle management. These changes made Moser Baer's active think tank ever more active and vibrant.

Composed of a diverse group of managers and nonmanagers, executives and technical staff, women and men, new employees and founders, the active think tank at Moser Baer took their task seriously. Having become a half-billion-dollar company in five years by that point, they needed a strategy that would help them to evolve and expand. And they needed to do so operating within a highly turbulent industry in an emerging market.

With that as the backdrop, Moser Baer's active think tank collaborated to develop a way to combat declining industry margins. What they came back with was a complete surprise to almost everyone, including Deepak Puri. They would join forces with Bollywood and enter the fray by distributing movies.

As in many parts of Asia, "pirating" movies, music, and software was rampant in India. Conventional wisdom said that most people did not wish to support the illicit pursuit. Still, buying legitimate copies of movies was simply unaffordable to individuals with an average income at the time. In order to solve this dilemma, and address their own compromised margins in blank DVDs, Moser Baer went to the movie studios and negotiated a new royalty structure for a select subset of films. Although they entered the home entertainment market as a late entrant, they chose to use a low-margin strategy with high volume. In fact, the plan was to make buying films cheaper than movie tickets and nearly as cheap as pirated DVDs.

Moser Baer innovated not only based on price but also in terms of their distribution model. The plan was to sell movies at every corner store, essentially making buying a DVD as easy as purchasing a can of Coca-Cola. At the time, no other distributor was able to envision movies as a mass-market item—they were always high end.

The strategy was very far afield from manufacturing blank disks; yet, in a country of over 1.2 billion film-crazy people, the think tank uncovered a huge opportunity. Rising disposable income, increasing penetration of hardware, a large and growing content base as well as hectic lifestyles all increased demand for home entertainment. By 2013, the company had acquired tens of thousands of movie titles and additional content in vernacular and Hindi language.

In summary, Moser Baer's active think tank devised a way to move the company up the value chain and away from blank digital media and the associated deepening pressure on margins. According to Puri, this is a solution that never would have seen the light of day if not for the active think tank. Its structure, diverse makeup, and strategic mandate make it uniquely qualified to address future problems in an innovative manner.

This is not the only idea to come out of Moser Baer's active think tank. Perhaps even more surprising than distributing content, they also made an aggressive entry into the photovoltaic industry by manufacturing solar cells and modules. Regardless of how that latest move pans out in the end, Moser's active think tank succeeded in devising several ways to strategically diversify the organization's core offerings without rebuilding the entire business.

One benefit of the Active Think Tank, an expansion tool, is that it brings more of the people responsible for execution into the loop on decisions. Peter Jayakumar, chief HR officer at Gati, explains how this works for implementing HR policies: "Before we implement any decision, we share the details with the SPG members. We wait for 48 hours for their feedback and based on this response, we move forward. The simple reason is that strategies, if they are to be implemented well, need to have a 'buy' from the users, especially from the field [as opposed to] the head office."[20]

Above and beyond any one idea, active think tanks can enable organizations to be ready for the future and prepared to meet the challenges and surprises that inevitably emerge over the course of conducting business. Importantly, they are a tool that CEOs can use to gain insight into how to manage effectively in a changing world. Bringing together a diverse group of functional specialists from across the organization or network not only provides cognitive diversity but also changes the nature of the dialogue. With active think tanks, the conversations are more likely to be honest because they happen with regularity and individuals feel a sense of responsibility. Trust and transparency take time to develop. When a unit head reaches out to someone in their group out of the blue, for example, that person may be inclined to behave like he or she is in the hot seat; however, informal think tanks, which are ongoing, are a means to informally empower people, create candor, and allow innovation to occur organically.

The Majlis of the Middle East. Another way organizations are building intellectual buffers, particularly in the Middle East, is through the custom of the majlis meeting described earlier. The majlis is a cross between a salon and a town hall gathering. It brings people with diverse perspectives together to discuss both retrospective and future-oriented topics. In most of the majlis meetings I have attended, historical issues are discussed in the first 15–20 minutes, often as a way to break the ice and make a connection to the current topics. The rest of the meeting is dedicated to addressing emerging issues and potential concerns.

A popular custom, the enduring popularity of this phenomenon guarantees that ideas travel quickly from one majlis to the next. Both good news and bad are conveyed in a majlis meeting. This convention helps address problems as soon as they arise. In countries such as Dubai, the heads of state learn what's important to the community by convening their own majlis, and the members of the community learn the ruler's perspective as well as those of their peers. Majlis in business are, by nature, action oriented. It is a way for anyone to come to management with ideas, suggestions, or potential concerns. In this case, people convene, pool their knowledge, and come up with solutions that everyone agrees to endorse. Part of the promise of the majlis model is that ideas from all quarters are taken seriously.

Structured as a semidirected open forum, the majlis allows senior and mid-level managers to share information and issues across a number of stakeholders. If used correctly, it can facilitate a powerful transfer of qualitative/subjective information about evolving issues and problems. This type of knowledge integration, from external as well as internal sources, is key to action when surprises require a fast response. It is yet another way to bridge formal and informal interactions and build learning into strategic planning.

The Art of Management: Momentum

Managing for the end result (compression) and building intellectual buffers (expansion) are two ways that organizations can absorb bumps in the road without sacrificing momentum. As with the other shock absorbers, this one, too, depends upon the judgment of managers. Like change in business, the art of management and the need to oscillate between expanding (people and options) and compressing (time and information) is a constant. In this case, the Momentum shock absorber makes it easier to manage conflicting ideas and interests.

All told, an end-versus-means approach helps executives manage the contradictions that are inherent in today's fluid environment. There is a great deal to balance: the informal and formal, speed and precision, results and process, strategy and execution, engagement and authority, and so on. Knowing what is set in stone (a company's overarching objectives plus values) and what is open to interpretation (the implementation strategy) allows individuals to make independent decisions that are a solid match with the company's intentions. Intellectual buffers help organizations manage contradiction by delivering a diversity of ideas. The wide-ranging group of people in an active think tank delivers ideas that would otherwise be beyond the purview of senior management.

These tools, as well as others in this book, allow for the integration of left- and right-brain concepts. Both are necessary, but neither alone is sufficient for absorbing the bumps and sustaining momentum along the road to success. It is the manager's judgment around when to compress and when to expand that makes all the difference.

5

Foresight

Getting Ahead of Change and Chaos

Arvind Mills is nestled in the epicenter of India's textile industry in the western city of Ahmedabad.[1] At the time of Indian Independence, in 1947, the city was known as the Manchester of the East, named after England's center of textile production during the Industrial Revolution. In those days there were over eighty-five clothing mills situated in and around the region, today there is just one—Arvind Mills. How did Arvind become the world's third-largest denim manufacturer when every neighboring competitor failed? Their success is due in large part to their unique process for strategic planning. This process has enabled them to look into the future with clarity and change course even in times of incredibly turbulent change.

Foresight, the fourth and final Strategic Shock Absorber, is about seeing bumps and opportunities in advance and having contingency plans at the ready. Foresight is also about seeing the present for what it is and being prepared to respond to the changing external environment. As the competitive terrain within an industry inevitably shifts, strategic plans need to do the same at a commensurate pace. When times are chaotic, for example, strategic planning needs to take on a more fluid tone in terms of change and experimentation. When they are stable, there is less pressure and more time to consider the options. Although the pace of change is variable, the need for constant adaptation and alternate strategies is ongoing.

Getting back to our driving metaphor, our mode of operating necessarily shifts when we go from a large motorway to a single-lane county road. We proceed at different speeds, pay attention to distinct formal and informal rules of the road, and expect dissimilar types of twists and turns depending upon the terrain. Still, we need to get to the airport on time regardless of the road, so we switch modes automatically and proceed accordingly in response to new conditions. Yet, we don't seem to be able to make this same switch in business. More commonly, we maintain the same mode even after we sense that the environment is shifting. Why? We consider a strategy to be sacred. When a CEO makes a strategy statement it calls to mind the biblical story of Moses coming down the mountain with the Ten Commandments. We don't use stone tablets in business. Instead, we print T-shirts and posters, and design slogans celebrating our grand plans. This type of pomp and circumstance makes it difficult to stand up and question the fully formed strategy without seeming out of sync or disloyal.

The tools introduced here, Strategic Assumptions and Alternative Strategies, help companies see more clearly into the future and make shifting strategies midstream more

Figure 5.1 The Foresight Shock Absorber

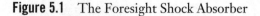

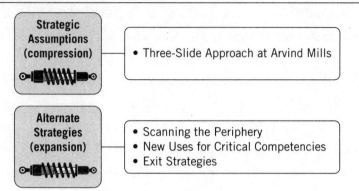

palatable. Strategic Assumptions, a compression tool, guides companies to focus on the archival information that indicates whether a plan can succeed. Alternate Strategies is an expansion tool that focuses attention on seeing what is new and next, as opposed to measuring interim progress toward a goal that will very likely shift before you can achieve it.

Strategic Assumptions

The denim producer Arvind Mills has had the same process for planning and capital expenditures in place for decades. It involves a few simple steps to which the entire organization adheres. With it, anyone from the GM on down to line managers can bring new business opportunities to the board for legitimate consideration, as long as they are able present the idea effectively in exactly three slides. These slides must adhere to a specific recipe that is to be followed exactly.

The first slide is an elevator pitch—a succinct summary of key requirements and merits of the idea. This is pretty standard in any organization. If you can't pitch the essence of an idea in a few bullet points you probably do not understand the key enablers of success and the leading sources of risk.

The second slide outlines the bare-bones financial projections: how much money is required and when; and how much capital will be generated in return and over what time frame. That does it for the financials—there are no complex presentations, spreadsheets, internal rate of return, currency exchange rates, and other variables that can be judged subjectively or used to shape the numbers. Arvind's financial team takes the simplified projections and crunches the numbers on their own, using consistent assumptions in order to avoid financial gimmicks and game playing that can be used to dress up projections.

The third slide is the most interesting and important. It contains what I call the *Strategic Assumptions*. These are the four or five critical enablers of the business idea under consideration. They are the specific baseline elements and events that must be in place for this particular strategy to succeed. These may include internal capabilities, such as technical knowledge or leadership; competitive factors, such as proprietary technologies; emerging industry dynamics, including mergers; looming trends, such as rising energy prices; legislative developments, including changing policies, quotas, or tariffs; and broad country-specific and global factors that may make the opportunity time sensitive. India's main commercial real estate developer, DLF, takes strategic context into account when they consider buying a parcel of land. If at any time during the due diligence process the price of the parcel is estimated to exceed one-tenth of the selling price, then they move away from the opportunity.[2]

Arvind's three-slide approach for evaluating new business opportunities is notable because it keeps the process fast, informal, and focused on the key elements of the proposal. There is minimal preparation time and the simplicity gives decision makers a clear view of the pros and cons. This type of process opens ideation up to the entire organization—anyone with a good idea is encouraged to step forward. If they can pitch it in the three-slide format the executive team listens with an open mind.

What is worth a closer look here is the third slide, Strategic Assumptions, because it systematizes something that is almost universally overlooked: the original context of an idea. Individuals who do strategic planning in most organizations are smart people with their eyes fixed on the future, yet they frequently fail to capture this original context. That is, they neglect to identify and track what the environment looked like (or what the future environment was expected to look like) when the idea was conceived. Think back to the US space program. When Stage One of a rocket was used up it was simply jettisoned away. The same holds true with strategic planning. We capture ideas but lose the original context that led the organization to believe the ideas were valid. Preserving the all-important original assumptions allows executives to determine whether a strategy remains applicable months or years later. It provides clarity around whether the plan still has a chance to succeed or if it should be scrapped altogether.

Arvind's approach to investments doesn't end once the idea has been formally approved and funded. Instead, the organization has a system in place to monitor strategic assumptions over time. The business unit leader works with the CIO (the

Chief *Information* Officer, not the Chief *Investment* Officer) to develop a dashboard monitoring each of the strategic assumptions. They set time aside to talk about changes in the environment and other shifts in context. Then, if and when they see that a majority of the stated assumptions are violated for an agreed-upon period of time, the company adjusts or abandons the plan. This is their decision trigger. They do not wait for the effects of a flawed strategy to manifest themselves in bad financial results that may show up years later; instead, they are empowered to act fast. This makes strategic planning proactive, not reactive. Monitoring strategic assumptions not only helps companies track what matters, but it also guides them to keep their eyes fixed on the changing external environment.

Over the years, managing and monitoring Strategic Assumptions has been the basis for Arvind Mills' ongoing success. For instance, one of their crucial assumptions during one of their planning cycles centered on the price of cotton. Cotton, which makes up 50 percent of the cost of producing denim, can exhibit wild price fluctuations. At the time, Arvind's executives anticipated that a significant price escalation was on the horizon, and they acted quickly on that assumption. In fact, they went so far as to rent every available warehouse space within a hundred miles of Ahmedabad, and they purchased enough cotton to fill every single warehouse. Their assumption panned out. The price of cotton skyrocketed and the company saved a fortune in raw materials. The move significantly improved their margins while most of their competitors lost a fortune and began their decline. Since then, Arvind has become accustomed to holding larger inventories of cotton when prices are low. The management has also explored options like forward trading, although this is not yet readily available in India. Today, the procurement of cotton has been separated from production. The type of cotton required is now described by the production team in terms of physical properties and is sourced from all over the world, inviting the best quotes possible.

The key point is that the projected price of cotton is a strategic assumption that drives Arvind's planning as opposed to tracking pure sales and revenue goals. The idea of strategic assumptions is important because it helps to make planning dynamic and proactive as opposed to reactive. It creates a trigger for change. Too often, when a strategy is developed, companies plan to measure progress through a set of interim milestones—the completion of a new plant, hiring staff, sales targets, profitability goals, and so forth. But these interim milestones may no longer be appropriate if the industry context alters significantly. The strategic context or competitive environment that the strategists originally envisioned is what really needs to be measured, because it signals the appropriate time for change.

In a business environment with frequent shocks and upheaval, companies need to acknowledge the painful reality that their initial strategy is very likely to be wrong. Developing foresight doesn't mean that we can ever really know with certainty what will happen next. Instead, it means that we should expect bumps to occur frequently and be prepared to implement the next appropriate response. Having strategic assumptions makes it possible to switch course when a flaw is found in the current plan or when industry dynamics shift.

Changing the System

Even with advance knowledge and foresight, changing a strategy course midstream is difficult. The lion's share of the dilemma centers on the fact that an executive's credibility is frequently associated with a particular strategy. Executives present their long-range plans for the future with confidence and authority, and endorse them in corporate off-sites locations and road shows. To admit that their plan is imperfect signals a miscalculation, which calls their leadership ability into question. Of course, this logic presumes that senior managers can see perfectly into the future every time. Until we can reframe the role of CEOs within an organization, and admit that the future is largely unpredictable, it is all but impossible for senior managers to frequently develop and publicly support alternative strategies.

Circumventing the myth of the perfect CEO requires two things: a change in process and a different mind-set.

Part of foresight involves knowing when to change. First, we need to step back from fixed approaches that paint strategy strictly as a sustainable long-term proposition. For instance, the five-year plan is an obvious example of a process that does not leave room for fast change. Increasingly, in today's competitive environment, many companies know they can't look years down the road with complete certainty, and yet they tether themselves to one plan for the duration. Every interterm milestone achieved—managers hired in year one, factory built in year two, and so on—creates a snowball effect that makes it more difficult to change direction. The solution, then, is to deemphasize the timeline. Monitoring strategic assumptions instead of dates on a calendar ties change to market conditions, rather than to an arbitrary point in time.

Second, we need to adopt a mind-set that allows executives to endorse change more readily. At present, senior executives are expected to sell one clear course of action and then stand by it with utter confidence. They need to project certainty so that others will climb on board. Conversely, a process that builds in options rather than anticipating certainty makes change feasible and transparent. It also takes away the stigma of being wrong. When the price of cotton was about to shoot up, Arvind Mills made a bold move because there was a process in place that made it possible and a mind-set that was open to change. Planning for change takes away the stigma and builds in a faster response time. In addition, it allows change without blame. Initially, everyone agrees to the plan; later, if the environment changes, the same individuals can agree to adapt.

Why is it that in some organizations employees don't ever raise their hands when they see a strategic problem? Because they will be blamed. Management asks: "How could this happen?" or "Who approved this?" To the contrary, strategic assumptions begin to create a no-fault culture. "We all agreed that these were the critical factors most likely to occur in the future. However, changes in the external environment that no one anticipates came about, causing the strategy to become irrelevant or invalid." Strategic assumptions create trip wires for change.

Textile and clothing manufacturing is highly competitive and vulnerable to frequent swings in the commodity pricing of materials, as well as to changes in technology and the global workforce. Arvind Mills needed their unique strategy planning process in place to proceed and succeed amid wildly challenging conditions. But think of so many other industries that are transforming rapidly, from media and energy to health care and education. These are industries where long-range plans are out of date before the T-shirts are printed and pressed. Planning for stability is no longer an effective

---

CREATING TRIP WIRES FOR CHANGE

- *Capture the original assumptions associated with a strategy.* Instead of laboring over every minute detail of your strategic vision, monitor what may change—particularly market conditions and other fundamental elements that need to remain intact in order for a strategy to succeed. In other words, keep an eye on shifting context as opposed to the static minutiae. Monitor the assumptions you made at the start that led you to believe that the strategy was a winner in the first place.

- *Make change safe.* Rapid adaptation becomes much more difficult when a fully formed strategy is canonized for the long term; or when high-priced consultants publicly endorse its efficacy. (How do you pay someone $200,000 for something that is wrong? You pretty much have to say it is right.) By acknowledging the reality that any strategy is likely to be temporary (a stepping stone to the next), you set the organization's sights solidly on the future.

- *Create a trigger for change.* Tools such as decision triggers and strategic assumptions add a dash of science into the mix without creating rigidity. They also minimize emotions by making change predictable and acceptable. There is no way to create a no-fail culture because failure is an integral part of business from which we can learn. However, these tools help to create a "low-fail" culture by focusing our attention on the things that really matter.

mode of operating. Organizations need to be ready when commodity prices skyrocket, competitors enter from a new space, or consumer preferences change completely. Like monsoon floods in India, these game-changing events are entirely common. And in business, these types of events are no longer a crisis; they are an opportunity to be the first to see the change and shift modes.

Alternate Strategies: Scanning the Periphery

Capturing the strategic context allows organizations to implement new strategies quickly when the terrain changes, rendering the current plan invalid. But how are alternate strategies devised? One simple and underutilized means of identifying the next best strategy is by scanning the periphery. The idea is to systematically sweep for opportunities that are adjacent to your own. These adjacencies come in many forms. Concept adjacencies, for example, are incrementally new ideas designed to suit your existing market, such as when towel maker Welspun expanded their business by producing sheets and rugs. But there are numerous other adjacencies to consider. Physical adjacencies are a chance to adapt an existing idea for a different locale. (Pizza Hut's move into rural markets.) Business model adjacencies deliver an existing idea in a new way. (Going from retailing to e-tailing.) Domain adjacencies lift an idea from one domain and transfer it into another. (Using a solution created in manufacturing to deliver health care, for instance.) Despite these and other categories of adjacencies, executives often limit their thinking to one type and neglect to harvest opportunities from the entire range. Systematically considering each of these adjacencies in turn can help identify your next new strategy.

Another means for scanning the periphery is finding new uses for your critical competencies or primary resources. Honda, for example, used their motorcycle engine to create a better chain saw. Scientists at 3M took a technology used to make highway signs brighter and applied it to hypodermic needles, making injections nearly pain free. A similar approach is identifying an organization's largest underutilized asset—and leveraging it. Karuturi Networks is a company that used this move to great effect.

Incorporated in India in 1994, Karuturi was a software developer and consumer Internet service provider. When these services took off more slowly in India than expected following the bursting of the dot-com bubble, Karuturi began looking for alternative ideas to put on the fast track. What they came upon was land—enough to let a thousand flowers bloom. In their original location, Karuturi had invested in property to develop a sizable campuslike facility, as many Indian IT companies (such as Infosys and Wipro) have done. With the new economy sluggish, the building was put on hold. Instead, they used the land to grow roses. It turns out that the climate, soil, and cost of labor made their location an ideal environment for rose production. The endeavor flourished (no pun intended) and Karuturi expanded further within India and internationally. They started out in technology and went on to become the world's leader in the production of cut roses. Today, Karuturi Networks produces approximately 555 million stems annually. It should be noted, as well, that Karuturi Networks is still in the business of software development and

ISP services. They have made both businesses—roses and technology—work for them.

Like the Strategic Wedge, scanning the periphery is an expansion tool that enables organizations to use their expertise to move into something new when the moment is right. Many times this is achieved by building on what an organization already has, be it a vital resource or a core competency.

The Indian "knowledge process outsourcing" (KPO) company Evalueserve[3] has made scanning the periphery one of their marks of distinction. Outsourcing, at one time, was a hotly debated term in the lexicon of business. As India's economy was emerging it (along with many other second-world countries) became a forerunner in the space. Launched in 2000, Evalueserve was one of the first to attract high-end non-IT outsourcing work and popularize knowledge process outsourcing in the process.

The brainchild of Alok Aggarwal, a former director for IBM Research Division, and Marc Vollenweider, former head of McKinsey Knowledge Centre, a captive unit providing research services to McKinsey consultants worldwide, Evalueserve provides customized research to help clients worldwide make decisions. Unmatched by any competitor, Evalueserve works in more than 190 countries, conducts approximately 170,000 hours of research every month, and has delivery centers in Chile, China, India, the UAE, the United States, and Romania.

Positioned as the "Flextronics of professional services," Evalueserve has evolved to cover five distinct service lines—business research, market research, investment research, intellectual property, and financial and data analytics. With these services as their broad foundation, Evalueserve's management constantly scans the periphery for opportunities to expand their portfolio. For example, they recently launched a new business line based on a sizable opportunity they identified while doing research for US medical insurers. As they went about that engagement, they uncovered and investigated what they believed was an opening to verify medical claims in the United States. Traditionally, only a small number of medical insurance claims are verified because of the high cost involved. But, in India, a dentist straight out of dental school often makes less than $10,000 per year. Evalueserve hired dentists straight out of university, paid them more than they would make in practice, and they then evaluated dental insurance claims. What started as an incremental move into an adjacent service has grown into a sizable business.

Scanning the periphery has enabled Evalueserve to adapt multiple times, fund their growth organically, and grow to over twenty-seven hundred employees.[4] They plan to continue to adapt and add new service lines; yet, top management is constantly grappling with strategic issues: Should Evalueserve incorporate products into its portfolio of offerings? What is the way to maintain the lead Evalueserve currently enjoys in the industry? Are there any unseen threats and strategies to counter them? How to become an international consulting juggernaut while avoiding channel conflict? Which new business lines to add? Essentially everything boils down to one open-ended question: where to go next? Scanning the periphery is how they answer the question.

Scanning the periphery has also worked for other Indian companies of note. India's premier commercial real estate company, DLF, also scans for adjacent opportunities. In their case, it looks more like focused diversification.

As described in chapter 2, DLF operates across seven overlapping real estate verticals. Although building office space was DLF's foremost venture, it was followed in 1982 by housing projects and in 1989 by community shopping centers. Shopping malls and organized retail space came into the picture in 2002. But the turning point for the company came in 2003 when DLF moved into hotels, Special Economic Zones (SEZs) and even infrastructure development such as highways and airports. There is no doubt that DLF has witnessed a meteoric rise in fortunes as a result of their expansion into adjacencies. Revenues for DLF grew 98.4 percent year after year from $139.5 million in 2005 to $280.9 million in 2006; the company's $2 billion IPO in 2007 was the biggest in India's history.[5] In 2013 the business was worth $1.7 billion, even after the rupee experienced a devaluation of 50 percent.

Saurabh Chawla, EVP of finance at DLF, explains their mode of rapid expansion across sector and geographic adjacencies: "We are aware of the changing environment and the rate of change. We are also aware of what we need to do, but since the speed of change is so high, we are constantly trying different means and methodologies to get on the bandwagon."[6]

DLF began in one concentrated area and scanned the periphery for ways to adapt and grow. This approach to growth is ingrained in the culture at many Indian companies. After all, much of the capital used to launch businesses in the region has traditionally been family money, so founders have a strong incentive to find new ways to grow and turn a profit. When one thing isn't working (even if it is their core business), they look to adapt to meet what the market really needs, as opposed to writing off losses. Sometimes this requires a total shift in strategic focus, such as when Karuturi Networks adapted their business from ISP services to cut roses.

Have an Exit Strategy

To some, scanning the periphery for alternatives while your current plan is in play may seem out of order. After all, one can argue that it indicates a deep lack of confidence in the original idea and diverts attention and resources. Yet, having an exit plan, or a way to get to what is next, is a fundamental part of managing and monitoring a strategy in a world of change. To some people this is obvious; and yet there is a psychological component that can make moving on very difficult.

Behavioral economists use a well-known experiment called The Dollar Auction to illustrate the difficulty of folding one's cards, even when it is clearly the very best decision. The illustration requires "auctioning" a dollar bill under certain provisos: the bill goes to the high bidder, but the two highest bidders must pay the last amount they bid. For example, if Player A bids five cents, and Player B bids ten cents, then Player B receives the dollar in exchange for a dime, and Player A loses a nickel.

Both players want to walk away with that dollar and avoid paying a loss—so they continue to up the ante. More often than not, momentum takes over and the game reaches a point where both parties bid 95 cents or more. With that, they each face the prospect of going over a dollar simply to minimize their loss. For example, if Player A bids 95 cents, and Player B bids $1, then Player A reasons: "If I quit now, I lose 95 cents, but if I bid $1.05, I can win the dollar and only lose 5 cents net."

This continues and the game escalates until the "winner" ends up paying well over a dollar. And the second player also loses a dollar or more. Clearly, it would be better to exit the game sooner—even if it means sacrificing the dollar.

Strategy is not necessarily a zero-sum game, but it is easy to fall into this same escalation mentality. We want to stay in the game longer because we have invested significant time and money in a certain game plan. Careers and bonus checks may be dependent upon success. Yet, in some cases, every day that we remain in the game the situation grows that much worse. Why does this happen? Often companies "ride it out" because of a lack of available strategic options. They need an exit strategy. The business lesson is to have a next plan long before the current one goes south.

How to Proceed Toward the Exit

The cardinal rule of planning should be something such as this: Don't assume that today is a good indication of tomorrow. The reality is that most traditional strategic planning starts by extrapolating based on the results of last year or last quarter. After that, considerable time and effort are spent creating quantitative goals and tracking progress. Yet, we know that finding that next strategy is just as critical as managing and monitoring current goals—perhaps more so for senior executives. Textile maker Arvind Mills, for instance, has switched up its strategy and product mix time and time again in response to sudden market shifts, often leaving interim benchmarks hanging. It started off making handkerchiefs; expanded when imported cloth was boycotted; revamped in the 1950s as technology developed; transformed itself from a multiproduct company to a denim manufacturer as government support for small mills hit bigger manufacturers in the 1980s; extended its line of products beyond denim in the 1990s; and in 2000, moved from being a commodity player to become a value provider and even launched its own brands.

Then, in 2005, after the United States lifted textile quotas, it found itself again actively looking for an alternate strategy. The sheer pace of change the development unleashed left Arvind executives with no precedent in a situation that was completely new and fluid. Growth in sales was not up to expectations, while denim prices crashed due to new investments leading to excess manufacturing capacities in the market. And China, suddenly a force to reckon with, immediately offloaded almost 40 percent of the world's denim supply into the international marketplace. With rising input prices alongside falling revenues, and with the literal doubling of competition and no one to blame other than the external environment, the underlying assumptions for doing business suddenly needed a serious relook. It is against this backdrop that Arvind moved further up the supply chain to become more closely integrated with select US retailers and brands.[7] Apart from its own brands, it now has moved into providing garment-manufacturing facilities to global leaders such as Levi Strauss, GAP, J. C. Penney, Banana Republic, Liz Claiborne, Nike, Reebok, Fila, and Walmart.

In Arvind's case, they owe much of their considerable success to turning plans on their axes and completely transforming themselves in response to the requirements of the day. According to Subir Mukherjee, who heads marketing for Arvind's Asia-Pacific business: "Goal setting is important but market fluctuations are so high that you cannot predict tomorrow. Every month you have to think of a new strategy on how to remain profitable in business."[8]

One way to operationalize this is to regard your organization's strengths in a new light. For instance, the best place to mine for an alternate strategy may be wherever your overhead is highest. Put another way: explore alternate methods for deriving value from critical resources or major investments. Although these resources may be plain as day, how to best utilize them may not be so obvious. In the case of Karuturi Networks, their large parcel of undeveloped land yielded their least expected business opportunity to move from technology into horticulture. In the case of Moser Baer, they were able to use what was literally piled up in their warehouses—blank CDs and DVDs—to move into content distribution Bollywood-style.

Too many CEOs believe that it is their job to devise and deliver the perfect strategy. But in an ever-changing world, the role of senior managers is not about being infallible. Their job is to set the standard of behavior for the organization by learning fast and reacting to change.

The Art of Management: Foresight

Strategic Assumptions are a *compression* tool. They minimize the time and information required to track crucial success factors and warning signs. They also offer clarity around whether a strategy is sustainable or if it is time to initiate a revamp. As we saw, if the strategic context has changed it is a solid indication that now may be the time to move on to the next phase. Finding alternative strategies, however, is all about *expansion*—more people opening up new opportunities. By scanning the periphery, executives have a clearer view of options in adjacent spheres—those that are close enough to seize quickly.

The Foresight shock absorber moves in the same fluid way that the others do—compressing, expanding, and moving back again. In this case, the shock absorber illustrates the cyclical nature of oscillation and the need for constant adaptation. We design a strategy and track the strategic assumptions that are associated with it. Then, when the context changes, it is time to put an alternate plan into place (based on new strategic assumptions). This occurs over and over again, oftentimes in rapid succession. The tools here enable executives to react quickly and respond to current market conditions.

Just as the tools within the Foresight shock absorber interact and overlap, all four Strategic Shock Absorbers are compatible with each other. They come together to form a discipline for responding to change that is nonlinear, complex, and multidimensional. The art of management lies in knowing which tools to use and when to compress time and information or expand people and options.

As we will see in the next three chapters, the companies in my research used all of the shock absorbers in the process of managing through uncertainty. With that in mind we will go on to take a holistic look at the model in the following way: chapter 6 examines the four shock absorbers together and further explores the dynamics of oscillation. Chapter 7 looks at the importance of guarding the one thing that remains the same even as the environment shifts dramatically—values. Finally, chapter 8 examines relevant management innovations that come out of India and other fast-changing markets.

As the global markets continue to homogenize, no single country or company is any less vulnerable to bumps and shocks or more able to access the opportunities that emerge. Because of that, the West can learn from India's example and Dubai's experiences during their spurts of intense growth, just as both have learned countless lessons from the West's history of growth and progress.

6

Execution

Shock Absorbers in Action

Harnessing the properties of the Strategic Shock Absorbers creates important new options for executives managing through chaotic change. And the power to truly transform an organization comes not from contraction and expansion alone, but from the two modes working together. The united forces of contraction and expansion can, in a sense, be compared to salt, which is made up of equal amounts of two chemical elements. Separately, sodium and chloride are fundamental elements, each with its own uses. Combined, they create a geometric pattern of alternating molecules that form a perfect crystal lattice and an ionic compound that is fundamental to life. Within the Strategic Shock Absorbers, when contraction and expansion are happening, either at the same time or alternately, the oscillation effect creates an energy that enables change and flexibility.

Compression and Expansion

Haier, the Chinese home appliance manufacturer and a leader in its market space is a state-owned company with three decades of business under its belt—an eternity in fast-moving China. Zhang Ruimin, its current chief executive officer, is widely credited with rescuing what was, in the 1980s, a dilapidated refrigerator company and turning it into a world-class organization. Ruimin is an innovator who had a vision for change that was based on quality improvement and process efficiency. To emphasize the need for change when the company was struggling and close to bankruptcy, Ruimin brought dozens of poorly made refrigerators down to the factory floor and distributed sledgehammers to employees. In a move that no one present would forget, he ordered workers to demolish the refrigerators and took the first swing himself. It was an iconic moment that defined the organization and established a corporate culture based on high standards and productivity. With a swing of the hammer he instantly changed the course of the organization. That is compression. Fast action, firm control, immediate impact.

Compression, of time, information, or control (or a combination thereof), creates a powerful lever for change. It is swift and sends a signal to employees and the market. Consider CVS, for example. You can easily bet that very few individuals were party to the decision when the pharmacy went cold turkey on tobacco products, forgoing $2 billion in annual revenue. It was a "the buck stops here" move that came directly from the C-suite and board of directors. And the decision was highly strategic. According to CVS pharmacy president

Helena Foulkes, CVS sees its future as "an alternative to the doctor's office."[1] In other words, their growth is in health care as opposed to tobacco sales. The best way for CVS to make the switch was in compression mode. They chose to act fast and unilaterally as opposed to creating a task force. The move made headlines, communicated the future direction of the company, and earned CVS kudos in one bold hammer blow.

In a turbulent, highly competitive environment decisions need to be made in an instant with extreme precision. Senior leaders assume command and live with the risk in order to deliver speed and control. When seven people in the Chicago area died from cyanide-laced Extra-Strength Tylenol, Johnson & Johnson's director, James Burk, acted in an instant to recall tens of millions of bottles nationwide. At a time when recalls were unheard of, J&J spent over $100 million in an act that potentially saved lives and ultimately preserved the Tylenol brand.

Expansion can be similarly powerful. Recall Karuturi, the software developer and Internet service provider that changed course to become one of the world's largest producers of long-stem roses. Or 3M, the Minnesota "Mining and Manufacturing Company" that now produces more than 55,000 products ranging from innovative adhesives to car care and dental floss. This is expansion. Making a smart move to change and grow in response to the current market.

We often think of technology companies when we consider fast change and adaptation. PayPal, Google, Facebook, and Wikipedia all iterated their business models multiple times before becoming blockbuster brand names. Yet, as we have seen throughout this book, established companies—from Zara and Pizza Hut to Arvind Mills and Network18 (discussed in chapter 8)—are just as apt and able to expand through iteration and adaptation. Expansion mode requires broad participation and buy-in from many people in the organization and that empowerment builds engagement and yields trust.

Compression (of time and information) and expansion (of people and options) can both be powerful, each at the right time and in the appropriate measure. Used together with oscillation, as we will see, they enable speed and control.

Figure 6.1 Oscillation: Compression and Expansion

Each shock absorber has two phases—*compression* and *expansion*. For each, the same elements are compressed or expanded. Time and information are always compressed. People and options are always expanded. This is part of the strength of the shock absorber model—it is robust and consistent.

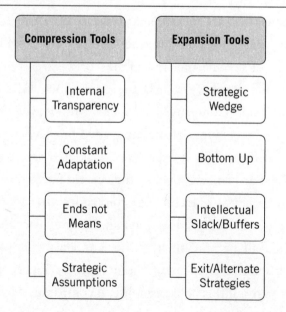

DLF's Strategic Shock Absorbers

India's independence and the creation of Pakistan in 1947 caused large numbers of people to cross borders and settle into areas which were hitherto uninhabited in India. Entrepreneur Chaudhury Raghuvendra Singh saw this as both a business opportunity and a chance to provide a necessary service to the uprooted masses flooding into the country. Today, only a handful of people realize that it was Singh who built the up-market residential colonies of Delhi years before he started Delhi Lease and Finance, better known today as DLF.[2]

Before DLF, all there was to see in New Delhi were large patches of barren land. The commercial real estate picture is markedly different now, with "DLF City" spread over three thousand acres, making it Asia's largest private township. DLF City incorporates massive office complexes, multistory residential towers, expansive retail spaces, and recreation and leisure zones.

With footprints at more than thirty locations, DLF is a dominant player in the Indian real estate market. As of March 2014, the company had three million square feet of leased retail space across the country.[3] The ambitious commercial real estate venture would never have taken off were it not for Singh's gift in the art of management.

Like many of the Indian companies in my study, DLF needed all four Strategic Shock Absorbers to secure their position as a landmark company navigating the turbulent terrain of the Indian economy. The strategic planning challenges in India were, until about 2011, the effect of corresponding growth opportunities that were rising at a brisk rate. The level of development and the pace of change made the nature of strategic planning in India an incredible challenge. More recently, growth in India has slowed, thereby continuing the cycle of change and chaos. The unpredictability in the business environment, first in India's high-growth phase and now as the growth rate becomes more volatile overall, makes India a sort of microcosm for the rest of the world, as businesses everywhere struggle with fast change and surprise market swings across the globe.

Expansion Mode

It was 1982 when DLF first ventured into residential housing and realized its importance as a leading bread-earner for the company. By March 31, 2007, DLF had developed more than 224 million square feet of colonies and townships, constituting 17 million square feet of residential property built by DLF. Their residential projects range from large middle-income group housing to leisure villas for which DLF handpicks its customers.[4]

Using their foothold in the residential colonies of New Delhi as a classic Strategic Wedge, DLF systematically expanded their business over the last quarter century. They spread out across multiple verticals (or business units), with their strongest segments being office space, housing developments, and retail leases. Building office space was DLF's foremost venture, followed by housing projects in 1982 and community shopping centers in 1989. Shopping malls and organized retail space came into the picture in 2002. These initial businesses, first created using a strategic wedge, set the stage for much more growth to come.

From there, DLF became expert at spotting opportunities adjacent to their native space. Scanning the periphery and entering into joint ventures allowed DLF to expand outward more recently—into hotels, special economic zones (SEZs), local infrastructure, and leisure development.

DLF formed an alliance with the Hilton Group of Hotels to jointly develop accommodations and serviced apartments in India. The first phase of the seventy-five-hotel joint venture was rolled out with other properties planned in Delhi, Mysore, Bhubaneswar, Bangalore, Hyderabad, Goa, and Kolkata. The hotels operate under various Hilton brands such as the Hilton Garden Inn, the Homewood Suites, and the flagship Hilton brand. DLF also extended their presence into special economic zones, infrastructure development, and leisure-related property development. At present, the company has several IT SEZs operational with others in the pipeline. Plans are afoot to build additional SEZs in the IT sector as well as multipurpose SEZs. Expressways, national highways, airports, pipelines, and harbors are also among the key areas targeted by DLF.

The ongoing expansion mode at DLF is enabled in large part by frequent strategic planning cycles and a willingness for constant adaptation. Both of these are built into the approach and culture. According to Sanka: "Planning [at DLF] is a non-stop process.... Over the last year, we have been adding to our holdings and at the same time selling some of our other interests. We have a strategic plan to achieve 50 million feet every year—but that could change. We are not bound to a number. According to the need of the hour we may take this target higher or lower."[5]

Their willingness to course-correct and shift strategies quickly is exemplified in how DLF managed its long-awaited IPO in 2007. Originally slated for April 2006, the IPO did not take off at first. At over 175 million shares and $2 billion, DLF's would have been India's largest public offering ever and the first of many coming from the real estate industry. Hence, the Securities and Exchange Board of India (SEBI) wanted to exercise utmost vigilance in approving the draft prospectus and they set strict benchmarks to ensure consistency of reporting. With that as the backdrop, there was an unanticipated delay in vetting DLF's issue documents. Moreover, during the period, the Indian capital market experienced a downturn. Thus, offer documents were withdrawn and the IPO was delayed. The unforeseen delays made DLF rethink their strategy and act fast.[6]

According to Saurabh Chawla, senior vice president of Finance and head of Investor Relations, "When such a situation arises you either wait until you can implement your plans or you find alternative ways to achieve them."[7] DLF proceeded to increase its borrowings and expanded in size. It used debt to leverage its IPO and swiftly repaid it once the IPO funds were in the bag. They found a way to fast-track their IPO and thereby maintain the momentum required to attract public investors.

Compression Mode

Because they are in the business of real estate development, DLF's strategic expansion over a lengthy period of time has been well orchestrated. Yet, DLF also manages to execute compression strategies, minimizing information and time, in service of efficiency and speed.

With the Indian economy still growing at a healthy rate, the real estate growth curve has some fewer troughs (and more consistent peaks) than other markets. However, due to cyclicality, market leaders in real estate are vulnerable to pricing bubbles and busts. In addition, when they find a suitable tract of land, developers in many markets must often act very quickly to secure it for themselves.

In order to guard against property risks, DLF managers across the board abide by their decision trigger for securing property: *The cost of acquiring land must be less than one-tenth of the selling price*. This decision trigger is an imperative within DLF and every employee recognizes its importance. It helps them manage risks and restrict potential losses caused by fluctuations in land prices. Overall it enables managers to make deal decisions quickly that accurately reflect DLF's goals and values. This same decision trigger has kept DLF out of the pricing wars and caused them to focus on volume in terms of buying large tracts of undeveloped land instead of cherry-picking smaller choice properties that would each require considerable management resources.

Another way DLF compresses time and information (and other resources) is by adhering strictly to their minimum debt strategy. Since its inception, DLF has grown by utilizing its development earnings and not merely its wealth of land reserves. Until 2003, DLF operated with minimum debt on its books, and accounting concepts such as shareholders' equity were conspicuous by their absence. Whatever small loans DLF drew were promptly paid in full, with DLF celebrating "Zero Debt Day" every couple of years. Since 2004, DLF has raised debt occasionally to finance projects at opportune moments.[8]

However, the company is still extremely cautious about the level of debt and follows a strategy of never completely leveraging itself. Even now, the company's net debt is below the industry norm.

Beyond resource management, DLF also puts compression into action by focusing on the ends as opposed to the means. Although they have a sophisticated planning tradition developed over time, DLF identifies its end goals but leaves the specific path to achieving those goals less demarcated.

According to Chawla: "We are aware of the changing environment and the rate of this change. We are also aware of what we need to do, but since the speed of change is so high, we are constantly trying different means and methodologies to get [there]."[9]

The compression mode, like expansion, is a part of DLF's standard operating procedure. Oscillating between the two creates structure while also allowing for a certain amount of flexibility.

Balancing Compression and Expansion

All successful companies need to manage the interchange between expanding people and options and compressing time and information. However, what can be trickier is practicing the two in tandem.

At DLF, strategic planning is driven from the top down and managed bottom up at the same time. Their management council (comprising unit heads, functional managers and the vice chairman) meets annually to determine financial targets. This top-down approach helps set the approximate revenue and profit goal for the coming year, which is then subdivided among the various business units after detailed discussion. Unit-specific financial targets, once decided at the annual council meeting, are the exclusive responsibility of the unit heads, even if that means realignment of initially proposed focus areas.

The top-down planning process is complimented by a bottom-up approach, because, as Chawla acknowledges, "A vision that is set at 10,000 feet should be the sum of expectations set at ground zero. This requires the strategic vision to be tested."[10]

With involvement from the middle management, every unit presents plans for the coming six months and explains the rationale behind its approach. The unit-centric reports containing balance sheets, profit and loss statements, and cash flow results go up to the management council, and are usually reviewed individually. Deviations, if any, from the original targets set by the management council are discussed amongst the respective unit head, the CFO, and the vice chairman during quarterly presentations.

A dual approach of a similar nature is visible throughout the various planning horizons at DLF and is affected to a large extent by external factors such as customer feedback. Planning is fine-tuned according to the findings that are derived from various customer groups and incorporated into ongoing projects.

Chawla explains: "Vision may be top down but the execution of that plan is bottom-up."[11] With that in mind, DLF works consciously to balance control and flexibility throughout the organization. Their structure is what makes this ideal achievable, with businesses organized into different verticals with disjoint structures. This formula clearly outlines the function, authority, and responsibility levels in different business segments.

According to Chawla, "Each business is run by a different CEO. They have their own financial teams but they don't raise their own capital. They utilize capital and manage their projects, and at the end of the day they pass returns on to the corporate entity (DLF Group). The corporate entity acts like a private equity investor—giving them the resources and demanding financial return on that capital."[12]

In addition, teams at each business implement projects without any intervention from heads of other verticals. They are assigned resources and provided timelines and given the flexibility to make decisions within established boundaries. These teams report to business heads from only one vertical.

Chawla explains, "My job at the corporate level is finding the requisite resources for the teams and planning on a yearly basis. These plans get fitted into the strategic plans on a three- to five-year basis. The project teams that are implementing the projects don't see the flux at the corporate level, so that they are fully provided for and they can implement their plans in a structured and controlled manner."[13]

K. P. Singh, who now occupies the position of a mentor for DLF, has become the public face for the company. Maintaining high-level government relations and performing nonexecutive functions is his new role. It is his son, Rajiv Singh, who has taken on overseeing the complex balancing act between expansion and compression. "The vision for the future is to be the largest real estate company in the world," Rajiv Singh told me.[14] Both Singhs are dedicated to managing the complexity of the chaotic Indian business environment by putting Strategic Shock Absorbers into full use.

The Upside of Oscillation

Oscillation is about speed, agility, momentum, and foresight—everything that the shock absorbers deliver. These are the capabilities that allow landmark companies in India and elsewhere to survive and grow despite the endless shocks and bumps that arise in high-turbulence markets. But there's more. There are three other things that the properties of oscillation deliver to companies that fortify and sustain them.

The first is a greater emphasis on the art of management. What I really mean here is that in fast-moving environments people are more important than ever. In creating a structure for balancing formal and informal controls, the Strategic Shock Absorbers empower individuals and redefine the role of the leader.

People are the primary resources for achieving strategic objectives. They are the adapters and adopters. The individuals that are closest to the market, and to customers, see new ideas and opportunities first. It is up to organizations to take this into account and create a truly integrated perspective. It is under these conditions (where bottom-up planning really matters) that the job of senior management fundamentally changes. Their job is no longer to initiate innovation by developing new strategies, but to realize the strategic potential of other people's ideas. They need to endorse innovation and then put their financial resources behind these ideas to scale them up across the entire organization.

Second, oscillation helps establish a culture of learning. Over the course of weeks and months you will hit more than one bump that threatens to sideline the business. As you compress time and information, and then later move back into expansion mode, you begin to benefit from the cycle. The oscillation of the Strategic Shock Absorbers enables you to ask questions like *what have I learned? Or, what will I do differently next time?* They create a step function that systematizes and consolidates learning. Part of the art of management, developed over time, is in knowing how quickly to cycle between compression and expansion. Wait too long and you are inefficient, switch over too quickly and you may minimize learning. What you'll see is that a small amount of money and time can yield a huge amount of knowledge and allow you to begin to understand the rhythm of the organization.

Third, oscillation is a way to integrate the formal and informal elements of strategic planning. This bridge between the structured and unstructured interactions accelerates communication and makes planning more effective—leading to the speed, fluidity, and accuracy described throughout this book.

Through oscillation, and the art of management, the Strategic Shock Absorbers enable speed—but speed is not enough. The final two elements we will examine are control and innovation. Control is managed by using values (examined in chapter 7) to guide actions, because values are the thing that remains constant. *Innovation* (chapter 8) is what enables organizations not only to endure constant change but also to benefit from it.

7

Driven by Values

Walmart, the sprawling multinational, and India's Future Group have some striking similarities. Both offer a wide array of consumer products from tube socks and tire irons to laundry detergent, pet supplies, and sporting goods. Walmart, the world's second-largest company, is far bigger in terms of size and scale, yet both are major employers that source items from thousands of suppliers. In addition, both own millions of square feet of retail space, sell to legions of customers, and base their business on value and deep discounts. Even their PR slogans sound alike: Walmart says they are "saving people money so they can live better." Future Group is "empowering local communities and fostering mutual growth."

These and other baseline similarities aside, the underlying values that steer each of these organizations are farther afield than Arkansas and Mumbai.

The mantra at Future Group is *rewrite rules, retain values*. The Indian organization wants to rise above established business norms to serve the Indian mass market without violating their guiding beliefs and ethics. One reflection of Future Group's value set is their unusual practice of *overpaying* suppliers. This stands in stark contrast to Walmart—a company that is legendary for squeezing every last nickel out of its partners. The price pressure they wield is relentless and designed to allow Walmart to pass the discount on to its customers.

Future Group bases their business on speed and response time. They believe that retail in India is the "business of the current." Therefore, they keep an ear to the ground listening for shifting consumer trends and changes in the marketplace. This applies to merchandise as well as the shape of their retail formats. In terms of inventory, only 70 percent of the product mix in Future Group's Big Bazaar stores is consistent across outlets.[1] Store managers stock the remaining 30 percent locally in response to consumer demand. Likewise, their retail concepts are designed based on what consumers want in the moment. For example, their Big Bazaar stores call to mind a traditional Indian marketplace, Brand Factories stock designer brand names, and HyperCity outlets are sprawling grocery superstores with aisle after aisle of produce and packaged goods.

With speed and response time as their primary driver, Future Group chooses to overpay vendors in exchange for preferential treatment and faster service. For example, if Brand Factories in Bangalore needs 850 Esprit scarves in a week's time, the goodwill they've built up through overpayment will help close the deal much faster and without a sky-high penalty or price tag. Thus, Future Group's means of hedging against environmental uncertainty is in sharp contrast to Walmart's approach. The latter, operating in a more stable competitive environment (within the United States, anyway) applies a strategy of cost minimization by squeezing suppliers. Pricing aside, Future Group believes they need to have products fast and first. The Indian market operates at a brisk pace, and if they don't oblige, their competitors will.

Despite the similarities, Walmart considers price to be its primary competitive advantage; at Future Group the advantages are speed and agility. These characteristics run deep for each of the two retailers and form the core of their values.

How Values Steer Strategy

We have examined a number of overlapping tools throughout this book that make up the Strategic Shock Absorbers. These tools enable executives to be more agile, adding new levers for moving quickly into strategies that suit the current environment. As we have seen, the role of these shock absorbers is to provide options for maintaining speed. They are like simple machines—they offer a significant mechanical advantage. Yet, accessing that advantage requires sound judgment. When time and information are compressed, the onus is on people to make smart choices. When the number of options and people expand, the very same is true—more people have greater latitude to act based on their judgment.

Good judgment is not something that is easily taught, but we can use parameters to guide our choices. How? By using values as a GPS. Future Group is guided by its core values when it overpays suppliers in exchange for faster service; likewise, Walmart is doing the same when it puts the screws to suppliers in order to provide lower prices for consumers.

Getting back to Mumbai's teeming traffic intersection, when you finally manage to pull out into traffic it feels like jumping out of the frying pan and into the fire. The morning commute is bumper to bumper, yet somehow it moves along quickly past construction, stalled vehicles, and bicycles gliding in the wrong direction. Taxis are honking at trucks and motorcycles while pedestrians walk in the middle of the road. Livestock is milling around, car parts are strewn in piles, and cars are parked everywhere. Driving in Mumbai is loud, exhilarating, and exhausting. The reality is that getting off the main thoroughfare is nearly as difficult as getting on. Remaining on course and arriving at your destination is fraught with complexity and traditional GPS devices seldom make it easier. For one thing, very few neighborhoods are laid out in grids. Therefore, people tend to navigate based on landmarks as oppose to cardinal directions. If you are not familiar with the landmarks, you are out of luck. In addition, physical landmarks change as quickly as anything else in India, so what was an alley a week ago may be a shopping center today.

In driving, as in business, we must navigate using something that remains consistent. In this case, that something is values. Values are a form of meta-consistency and a means for achieving a desired behavior across a variety of situations. After all, in fluid environments it is possible to burn up all of your effort in developing skills that are applicable in only a few situations. Instead, organizations need to use capabilities that transcend any single situation and guide behavior in many or most situations. Values make that possible.

The modern US military is a prime example of an organization that purports to hold tight to its values. Over time, their values have become ever more critical as their operating conditions have become much less predictable. During the more than forty years of the Cold War, for instance, the United States considered the Soviet Union to be its one constant "enemy." Thus, the comparative predictability or stability of their environment was relatively high. With just one main foe, the type of engagement was fairly standard: large-scale tactical strikes. However, with the fall of the Soviet Union in 1991, the nature of military conflicts changed dramatically. No longer was there one principle enemy. Multiple small tactical engagements sprung up around the world—the Persian Gulf, Somalia, Haiti, and Yugoslavia, for starters. These engagements each required differing capabilities—more ships, more ground troops, specialized intelligence, and so forth.

Even more fundamental than the conflicts themselves, soldiers' capabilities needed to evolve because of the increased variety of situations in which they found themselves. Hunting for plainclothes enemies in villages dominated by civilians is no simple task, particularly when adversaries can fire from almost any house or rooftop. As a result, the US military evolved. Basic training was no longer about adhering to a set of standard operating procedures and blindly following orders. The majority of training today is about instilling a set of values. Why? The operating environment is no longer homogeneous and predictable. By adopting a set of common values that are applicable across a variety of circumstances, organizations can adapt their actions (within the value set) to suit situations as they change.

Companies, like the military, talk about their values. It's not uncommon for an organization to indulge in navel-gazing about corporate culture. They may refer to values in a mission statement or during the on-boarding process for new hires. Yet, in most cases values are trappings. They don't actually play a major role in strategic planning. Like the US military during the Cold War, many Western companies have become accustomed over time to operating based on process and precedent. When conditions are relatively stable, it is easy and often appropriate to fall into a comfortable rhythm.

I would argue that companies accustomed to operating in fast-moving markets are the ones more apt to rely on values to steer strategy. For decades the high-tech sector, for one, and in particular computing, has been the poster child for rapid change and transformation as Moore's Law continues to call the shots. Companies such as Apple (think different) and Google (don't be evil) famously and publicly try to remain in sync with their values. In environments with little or no market transparency, values provide the basis for action. At organizations like Facebook and Zappos, for instance, values play a major part in hiring decisions. Why? Because values are too difficult and time consuming to teach to new hires. Many times, entrepreneurial organizations prefer instead to find people with the right mind-set (or value set) and then bridge any technical gaps with training.

During my research in fast-moving markets, I saw the very same thing play out in India and Dubai. Every one of the companies in my study considered values to be a cornerstone of strategy creation and execution. Evalueserve designed their strategic planning process around values. Arvind Mills used their core values to create a competitive advantage. Gati launched a company-wide transformation based on values. And so on.

Figure 7.1 Making Strategy Stick

Values . . .

✓ Guide an organization like an internal GPS.

✓ Create consistency during turbulence.

✓ Flexible enough to be embedded across activities and processes.

✓ Broad enough to suit situations across the spectrum.

✓ Can be used as a platform for change and transformation.

✓ Connect companies and customers.

Today, as companies in every industry discover rapid change around every corner, values become a main driver of strategy. We will look at why in greater detail and examine how the companies in my study used values as an integrating mechanism to make change manageable in high-growth turbulent environments. Values, and a culture that appreciates them, are the most important tool of all for making strategy agile and creating a foundation for the Strategic Shock Absorbers. Because values remain a constant backdrop, they enable companies to decode a changing environment.

The Value of Values

Values in business are sometimes seen as soft and secondary today, with negligible payback, when attention and resources are divided in more directions than executives can reasonably track. Yet, it is exactly that qualitative (soft) aspect that allows values to stretch and deliver hardcore benefits. As we examined throughout much of this book, the combination of formal and informal strategy processes allows strategy to be more flexible in terms of allowing companies to glide over bumps in the road. Let's look at why this is the case.

Values Dovetail with Competitive Advantage

The companies I examined closely in formulating the research for this book had several things in common. One of the most basic was that they considered their values to be part and parcel of their primary competitive advantage.

The most obvious example of this came from Arvind Mills,[2] a company established in 1931 to cater to the demand in India for fine and superfine fabrics. At the time, the textile industries of the UK and its Indian dominion were interlinked by necessity because most regions of India were colonized by the British. As a result, almost all of the high-quality cloth available in India was manufactured in Britain by modern power looms and mills and imported. That began to change during the recession of 1929, when Mahatma Gandhi championed the boycott of imported fabric by Indians under what was known as the Swadeshi Movement. With that, the Lalbhais family, founders of what came to be known as the Arvind Mills, saw an immense opportunity. They reasoned that the demand for imported fine and superfine fabrics, which were now being boycotted, could be satisfied if they were manufactured in India by Indians.

The Lalbhais set up the most modern integrated cloth mill of the time in Ahmedabad, India. It was one of the few mills that incorporated all the facilities, from spinning and weaving to dyeing, bleaching, finishing, and mercerizing. In other words, raw cotton fiber could be spun into yarn, woven into cloth, dyed with the color of choice, and finally finished as per requirements, all at one place with the help of modern equipment.

Hence, Arvind's core value of quality above all was born and became the basis for their competitive advantage, then and now. Every strategy that Arvind adopts is ultimately in service of that value. Arvind executives will be the first to say that quality is the main reason they are the sole survivor (and one of the world leaders in denim production) operating in a region where over eighty-five mills once operated. Still, despite their position of strength in the industry, Arvind has seen more than its share of challenges in what has long been an immensely turbulent industry. The changeover from hand to power looms is an example of one significant bump in the road.

Before the 1980s, the Indian textile manufacturing industry used mostly manual handlooms. During the 1980s, however, small manufacturing units using power looms to create fabric at a lower price became abundant, to the detriment of players such as Arvind. Power looms were less regulated by the government and sold their products at a lower profit margin due to their low-product differentiation. They had almost no overhead, such as R&D, whereas full-fledged mill operations such as Arvind spent 5 to 6 percent of their sales on research and development. At the end of the day, power loomers could sell their fabric much cheaper than the large mills. Compared to the mills, their scale of operation as well as their capital investment was much smaller. The minimum number of people required to start a power loom is only one compared to a mill which requires scores of workers even if it is set up on the smallest scale. Arvind Mills employs over twenty thousand.[3]

All of this gave power looms much more flexibility as well as the ability to handle small order quantities. As a result, they garnered a large share of the market. Although Arvind Mills managed to be profitable on the strength of its brand name and its commitment to quality, it understood that this was not sustainable. As a result, it decided to revamp its strategy while holding fast to its quality mandate.

Arvind Mills called the new strategy Renovision: *"A new way of looking at issues, of seeing more than the obvious."* This became the corporate philosophy. Under this strategy, Arvind Mills decided to focus on the international market instead of the domestic market. The main reason was that the international market (mainly the United States) expected and accepted only quality goods—fabrics manufactured accurately according to technical specifications along with timely deliveries.

These two requirements meant that the manufacturer would have to invest in capital-intensive technology on a large scale, as well as in better management of operations. Power looms could not match up with the technology and the scale required for quality control, logistics, and automation. Another factor that fueled their strategy was the shift in demand from synthetic fabrics to cottons. Above all, the Renovision strategy focused on high-quality premium niches instead of the popularly priced segments.

According to Ajit Mantagani, the CEO of Arvind's denim business, "The evolution of the Renovision strategy witnessed many changes to the company—to almost all the 7-S of McKinsey's famous model—Structure, Systems, Style, Staff, Skills, Strategy."[4] Nearly every aspect of Arvind was changed except Shared Values. Two values—delivering the best quality and continuous adaptation to the changing business environment—remained the same.

Subir Mukherjee, who managed marketing for Asia-Pacific, described Arvind's later decision to enter the denim market full-force in the 1980s as another attempt to dominate with product lines with high-entry barriers and quality standards. "Denim requires much higher process control. You have to assume what is going to be the usage of the product. Denim has to be necessarily washed. Different types of washes give different types of effect. So, when different types of customers wash it in different ways, it has to behave in a very predictable fashion. Therefore, denim has to have very standardised properties achieved through very high quality and process controls."[5]

Their focus on quality as their primary competitive advantage is an ongoing point of pride at Arvind. One of the workers on the Arvind campus told me: "Even our factory seconds (i.e., defective or rejected fabric) fetch a higher price in the domestic market than the fresh denim fabric from any other mill."[6]

It makes sense that core values and a company's source of competitive advantage should be interwoven, but this is far from the norm. As markets change with new competitors and entrants, established players oftentimes react to disruption in one of two ways. They either grasp at straws to update their strategy, with little or no regard to their core values and capabilities, or they hold fast to what they know best even as the environment changes around them. As Arvind Mills shows, the right values are flexible enough to support innovation and strong enough to remain constant as goals and capabilities change.

Values Can Be Embedded across Activities and Processes

An advantage of bringing core values into strategic planning is that they are broad enough to suit situations across the spectrum.

Evalueserve, the India-based "business knowledge out-sourcing" firm discussed in chapter 5, is a decentralized organization where analysts work in teams to conduct cutting edge research and provide custom analytics for clients in life sciences, finance, and professional services. According to Mohit Srivastava, AVP of business research, employees across the board at Evalueserve rely heavily on the firm's values to conduct their work. In large part, this practice is exactly what makes their flat structure efficient. Individuals are on point to call the shots for themselves, Srivastava says, but corporate values are fully embedded in their activities. These values, embodied in the day-to-day operations, are very specific:

- *Quality*: Providing the highest quality in every client inter-action
- *Confidentiality*: Guaranteeing the highest standards of confi-dentiality to customers
- *Integrity*: Being fully committed to customers and building enduring, trust-based relationships
- *Meritocracy*: Rewarding performance and fostering excel-lence
- *Obligation to Dissent*: Empowering employees to voice their opinions[7]

These ideas are broad enough to provide flexibility, allowing individuals to innovate without compromising what matters most to the organization. Though each of these precepts are deemed important, *quality* and *confidentiality* form the basis of Evalueserve's entire operating model. Back when they were first getting started, the founders realized that the only way to ensure uniform quality and confidentiality in a company full of brilliant individual contributors was to develop both formal and informal procedures around them.

As a result, the quality standards set up by Evalueserve are among the best in the KPO industry. Its processes have a built-in feedback mechanism to trace any abnormalities. For instance, benchmarking is performed on a wide variety of issues, including accuracy of research, structure and format of the deliverables, turnaround time, project management, and responsiveness to client queries. To further maintain consistent offerings, the company espouses "four-eye" quality checks (self-quality check, peer-to-peer quality check, project manager quality check, and editorial quality check) of all the documents. Other quality cross-checks include audits; weekly reporting—productivity report, exception report; weekly operation review calls—monthly governance calls; and many other review procedures. Finally, to further ensure quality, Evalueserve encourages its employees to attend various training programs and seminars.

Their second core value, confidentiality, is just as crucial in allowing Evalueserve to maintain their leadership position in the KPO domain. With that in mind, the company has put into place a system called the Evalueserve Confidentiality Management Systems (ECMS). ECMS encompasses several procedures related to the legal, technical, and operational arrangements of the organization:

A dedicated-unit: By setting up a dedicated team at its operational site, only team members have access to confidential data.

Client proprietary: Every project is customized according to client requirements and problem definition. Thus, the deliverables are considered to be client proprietary. In addition, Evalueserve religiously follows the practice of not sharing the key takeaway or the deliverables, even across their own teams.

The legal environment: All contracts are signed under the client's favored jurisdiction, primarily Western (United States or Europe). Confidentiality documents are signed with clients, and Evalueserve employees sign a nondisclosure agreement (NDA) that clearly outlines the dos and don'ts involved therein. The company also provides the right to perform audits to verify the company's compliance with the confidentiality agreements.

Technology: Evalueserve follows technological procedures to prevent breaches of confidentiality. Secure transmission, secure storage, and data access for team members only (on a need-to-know basis) are some of the focus areas that ensure information protection.

Culture: Evalueserve inculcates high ethical and professional standards in its employees. To ensure absolute confidentiality, the company does not staff the same employee to work on requests from competitors, for the period of time specified in the confidentiality agreement.[8]

These fairly rigorous operational systems ensure that the core values at Evalueserve cut across the entire organization. Importantly, they work in large part because they are balanced by an informal reporting structure with very few layers of hierarchy. In general, managers maintain an open-door policy where job title is not seen as a barrier to entry. Employees are incentivized to discuss problem issues and raise flags. This balance of the formal and informal infuses a sense of belonging (we are in this together) and motivates employees to maintain a holistic viewpoint.

Although their operational processes are specific to Evalueserve and the KPO industry, the takeaway is that qualitative values can be put into practice using quantitative means. In this case, the balance of the formal and informal allows Evalueserve the flexibility to innovate on an individual basis without sacrificing the values that make them successful.

Values Create Consistency during Turbulence

The Indian news station NDTV offers a glimpse of a company that has stubbornly anchored their strategy to their values in order to create a degree of stability during times of rapid change and development.[9] Like many of the firms profiled in this chapter, NDTV's point of view reflects their experience growing up in India's high-growth era over the last several decades.

Although the very notion of democracy was once dismissed by the colonial British as a far-fetched ideal that a poor, divided, and stratified nation of four hundred million was daring to dream, India today is seen by many as a fine example of democratic principles in action. In fact, the emergence of NDTV as India's leading news media house with a bouquet of news channels arguably underscores the maturing culture of democracy.

"The story of NDTV is the story of India," says the popular and charismatic chairman of NDTV, Prannoy Roy. "We grew as the bureaucratic controls declined and the voice of the people started to take an independent course."[10]

Of course, with democracy comes competition and NDTV is far from alone in Indian news media. The increase in the number of players is putting pressure on the entire industry to seek new ways of generating revenue. As a result, news channels are vulnerable to compromising the quality of their content in favor of sensationalism in order to gain viewership. This is especially true in the case of Hindi news media. According to Prannoy, there is ample revenue available for news organizations that decide to go the Bollywood route of celebrity programming. But this is not a path that would work for NDTV, an organization known for serious journalism. Prannoy says that following their values has meant exploring ways to grow as a business without diluting their core competence of serious news journalism.[11]

K.V.L. Narayan Rao, managing producer and CEO, told me that the organization has reinvented itself twice, both times maintaining its mandate for serious news. They started by producing exclusively international content for the national television news channel. "From there, we made international deals and started producing India-oriented news for the BBC. Going one step further, after the liberalization of the media industry and emergence of cable television, we started producing daily half-hour news bulletins for a prime-time private broadcaster—Star TV. We then took our alliance with the Star TV to a new level when we started producing content for their 24-hour news channel."[12]

NDTV continued to grow all the while in number of employees, news bureaus, revenue, and finally, in terms of public confidence in their programming. They became known as the independent and trustworthy supplier of quality news across the country. According to Rao, their solid focus on core values allowed them to differentiate their brand of serious TV journalism in a market crowded with lowest-common-denominator programming.

A key element of their values-based strategy has been to go to market as a pay channel as opposed to one that is aired for free with advertising support. This means that NDTV expects to draw its revenue from channel subscriptions as opposed to ad sales. This path suits their values, Prannoy says, because "we have consciously decided not to run after eyeballs. As a serious news channel, we do not think we will be able to match the viewership that general entertainment TV channels are able to achieve. We also do not want to compromise our [distinctive] synthesis of news and journalism to make it sensational."[13]

There is another angle to becoming a pay channel. Prannoy says: "Two critical things in the news business are independence and integrity. If we focus on advertisement sales as our main source of revenue, one of the areas of growth will be featured content. We would not like to do a news programme to promote any product or business or other private interests. This may affect our news quality and in the long run will also not make business sense as we will lose confidence of our viewers."[14]

All these issues are reflective of how NDTV is responding to the challenge of marrying good business sense without losing focus on its key values of good journalism. This is, by far, the biggest challenge faced by the company after becoming a telecaster and listing its stock on the equity markets. To make it work, they have adopted structural measures to ensure that business does not overrun news. For example, all of the news businesses have CEOs who are responsible for the strategic and financial performance of the channel, but all of them also have a managing editor. The ME's authority is on par with the CEO and both work together to make decisions. "Such a structural approach to safeguarding our short and medium-business interests and the long-term vision of who we are, will be a key to ensuring our success," Prannoy points out.[15]

NDTV is essentially turning down revenue in order to stick with the values that define their business. Still, executives at the news organization believe firmly that NDTV will succeed *because* of their focus on values, not despite it.

Values Are a Platform for Change and Transformation

Through the example of NDTV, we have seen that values are a cornerstone for keeping business consistent in fast times, but they can also be used as a platform for change. As most of us know from experience, one of the trickiest elements of any corporate transformation is adapting the culture. This is a complicated objective even in stable times. Although values are the one thing that remains constant even when the outside environment is in flux, when a company needs to change from the core, then values are instrumental.

Gati, the Fed-Ex of Asia Pacific described earlier, spent considerable effort grappling with this issue in 2006 as they brought their logistically complex business up to date at a time when the growth rate in India was 9.3 percent.[16] During their transformation, Gati's stated values centered on the promise of *a safe and timely delivery* of packages—no small feat in a country where the primary transportation infrastructure is still in development even today.

Increasing competition from global companies moving into the Indian logistics industry was a contributing factor behind the necessary overhaul. Through their makeover, management wanted to connect with customers and project Gati as a technology-driven company offering top-quality services. As part of the change they underwent a rebranding exercise, abandoning their familiar yellow-green uniforms in favor of turquoise. The company also adopted a new logo and adapted its tagline from "We deliver anything, anywhere" to "Ahead in Reach." The general consensus from Gati management was that they needed to reexamine their business right down to their core values in order to remain a leader in the changing competitive environment. As part of that, they had to reassess not only how they served their customers but also how they saw themselves.

According to Rajeev Chopra, then Gati's country manager of international business, the transformation had everything to do with values. "We not only changed our logo and colors, we also changed our corporate philosophy and the thinking behind it," he said.[17]

Keying in on the culture at Gati made the systems piece of the update much easier to enact because everyone was on board with the shift. With that in mind, Chopra describes the transformation as a "unified effort on the part of employees and management," and not merely something handed down by the board. He noted that the change was catalyzed by the lower hierarchy by way of feedback and suggestions. "It was a cultural change. We went down right to the grassroots . . . to all employees across all levels."[18]

The change initiative took a little over a year from planning to execution. In the end, their core values and the identity they projected to customers needed to reflect Gati's reach, its technological advantage, quality of infrastructure, and the overall caliber of its people. With that in mind, the updated brand was accompanied by a new set of corporate values that spoke of "Domino Discipline," which was a nod to combining reliable delivery and process control.

The transformation went ahead and today Gati is an over $200 million[19] company reporting double-digit revenue growth in the first half of 2014.[20] Now, as then, the company readily acknowledges that their values help them remain agile and relevant. To that end, Gati conducts regular employee satisfaction surveys to collect inputs on the company's processes and policies. Externally, customer satisfaction polls are also conducted with the help of third parties. Before undergoing the corporate transformation exercise in 2006, these same company surveys helped Gati understand customers' requirements and develop the set of corporate values that still drive the company forward today.

Values Connect Companies and Customers

In the heyday of CDs and DVDs, the Indian tech manufacturer Moser Baer designed its core values around what they knew their customers needed most: quality and reliability. Adopting values with customers in mind delivered for them on two levels. Externally, they say it enabled them to remain competitive for years in a crowded, fast-moving industry. Internally, it allowed them to use their values as a litmus test for important strategic decisions.

Executives at Moser Baer talked to me about the early years at the company and explained why Moser's values brought them closer to customers in the days prior to flash drives and cloud computing.

Chief Operating Officer Girish Baluja said: "The industry at the time was dominated by large Japanese and European competitors. They were the biggies and we set out to penetrate the club. On top of that, Moser Baer was based out of India—a country not known in the global market as a high-quality manufacturing hub." Vivek Chaturvedi, chief marketing officer, adds: "The challenge began right from making the basic disc to packaging it in a retail-ready form. It required a complete breakdown of our people's habits. . . . It required a cultural change."[21]

Moser was able to use its values to exceed these barriers to entry. A big hurdle was securing its first major order. According to Deepak Puri, Moser's founder and chairman:

I was told by the Germany based BASF's magnetic division [now defunct] that doing business with an unknown Indian company was not something they were keen on. I told them: "Just give me a rolling forecast and your word that if you find me [reliable] month to month, if the product is of international quality and if you find me competitive, you might think about buying from us. I will ship it directly from India, store it in our warehouses in Europe and ship it to your warehouse at your command so that you can have zero inventories. Further, I will give you 90-days' credit from the date of shipment and if your customer took 60 days credit from you, you will still be sitting for 30 days on my money." I was that confident about the value additions I could give to them.[22]

Moser Baer went on to build its business model on catering to the world's twelve largest original equipment manufacturers. With this, Moser earned an 18.5 percent global market share in 2005, back when CDs and DVDs were a thriving and competitive industry.[23]

Beyond closing deals and fueling customer retention, their focus on customer needs guided Moser in its planning. One important element of their quality strategy was near-complete "vertical integration in both directions." What this meant was that product packaging—back then cake boxes and jewel cases—was produced in house. At the time, many of Moser's competitors outsourced labeling and packaging. Moser manufactured everything themselves in order to manage the quality. For processes that were outsourced, Moser trained vendors themselves, installed quality systems and processes, and required environmental safety certification.

Moser Baer believes that their customer-centric values played a role in transforming the "Made in India" label into something to be proud of. There is no doubt that it is part of why it led Indian hardware manufacturing at a time when the world's attention was on software. And it garnered a leadership position without complaining about the infrastructural drawbacks of being based in India.

Creating a Culture Where Values Matter

Values matter for the reasons mentioned here as well as many more. All of the companies I worked with throughout my research truly valued values. Even with so many vastly different stories and situations, I found many commonalities that offer general guidelines.

First, values need to be simple to understand. In order to benefit most from values they must be clearly communicated and widely apparent internally and externally. At Ferrari, for example, speed comes first, and it has been so at the company from the very beginning. It is a transparent value that employees build into everything from product design and R&D to advertising. Ferrari began as a manufacturer of racecars and it participates in racing in an ongoing way, especially Formula 1, where it has had considerable success. Some would say speed is a value that Ferrari flaunts. Externally, car consumers pick up on that and perceive Ferrari as a symbol of speed as well as luxury and wealth. It is clear that the company and its consumers alike consider this to be a point of distinction. In many ways, speed defines Ferrari, and that is the reason this core value delivers so much to the organization.

Next, values need to be top down. We saw that the mantra at Future Group is *rewrite rules, retain values*. With that in mind, management there created a chief executive–level position—CEO of Innovation and Incubation. This role sends a message to the entire organization that innovation is of crucial importance to everyone at Future Group. At many companies innovation is managed informally, with experimentation happening occasionally at the periphery on an ad hoc basis. According to Future Group's managers, they do not want to stifle informal innovation, but adding a C-suite role helps to formalize the informal and sends a strong signal to everyone within the company that management supports innovation.

But values also need to be bottom up. Looking through a grassroots lens, values create a positive ends-versus-means dynamic, enabling people to understand bottom-line priorities and act accordingly. Although terrains change, values generally do not; however, this positive effect requires trust and empowerment. People need the latitude to make decisions fast and on their own without undertaking a lengthy process. This puts the onus on managers to hire people who are a solid fit in terms of their values. Senior executives can't always tell people exactly what to do. Values define the legal playing field, and employees have the latitude to implement strategy accordingly.

All of these things point to people as being more important then ever. You can teach someone rules and give them tools but values are ingrained. They require a different type of buy-in that comes from within.

We said earlier that cars have brakes to enable us to drive faster. If the only way to stop is by crashing into something, then the response will be to move along very slowly. Similarly, shock absorbers enable cars to speed across bumpy terrains. But values go beyond speed to offer precision and direction. As an organization's internal GPS system, values are the stabilizing mechanism that enables shock absorbers to deliver their benefits. They establish a shared reference point for making decisions. When people are on the same page, they can use that common understanding to respond quickly with confidence. Like the shock absorbers themselves, values facilitate oscillation. In this case, when people and options and other critical resources expand and then contract, values stay constant in order to create the stability that companies need to remain intact during times of incredible change.

8

Management Innovation from Fast-Moving Markets

Companies featured throughout these pages have important commonalities. Arvind Mills, Dabur, Future Group, DLF, and Network18 (discussed later in this chapter) are not only leaders in their respective industries, but they are also united by a keen ability to perceive and react to change without letting organizational egos get in the way. In that sense, they are emblematic of many other Indian companies. There is no other way to have survived the last two decades in the maelstrom that has been India other than by embracing strategies that absorb shocks and convert them into positive change. From riding the euphoric highs to losing their footing in a free fall, to every conceivable condition in between, these and other iconic Indian companies offer lessons for the rest of world, which today experiences all of the same frequent shifts and chaotic changes.[1]

Sanjay Lalbhai, chairman and managing director of the $1 billion[2] Arvind Mills group still notices the empty chimneys piercing the skies of Ahmedabad, once called the Manchester of the East. Now, this sole survivor is the largest manufacturer of denim in India and the fourth largest in the world. Its success mirrors the story of modern India: a series of false starts and bold steps followed by a triumphant emergence and then a few steps back. Along the way, Arvind Mills has constantly reinvented its strategy and product mix in order to put itself one step beyond the competition. They started off making handkerchiefs; expanded when imported cloth was boycotted; revamped in the 1950s as technology developed; transformed itself from a multiproduct company to a denim manufacturer as government support for small mills hit bigger manufacturers in the 1980s; extended its line of products beyond denim in the 1990s; and in 2000, moved from being a commodity player to become a value provider and even launched its own brands. More recently, when denim prices fell, Arvind Mills moved into providing garment-manufacturing facilities to a bevy of global retailers.

As an organization, Arvind is always proactive and constantly changing every time its assumptions about markets and consumers are violated. In India, tales of dramatic organizational adaptability and rapid growth are legion. Think of Infosys' remarkable growth, from beginning life in 1981 funded by $250 to its current revenues of more than $5 billion.[3] Think of Tata Industries' restless reinvention from a steelmaker to a globe-spanning conglomerate. What links these remarkable feats is a distinctive Indian approach to strategy, one that enables strategies and organizations to constantly adapt as the world changes.

As Vivek Chaturvedi, vice president for international marketing at Moser Baer, one of India's leading technology companies, puts it: "In India, it's about thriving in chaos. We have been taught how to do business the Japanese way, the American way and the German way. We have always thought there is an Indian way of doing business. After you've grown from a $50 million company to a half-billion-dollar company, you develop a character—and it is developed due to the environment in which you operate. It is very difficult to try and internationalize yourself. Instead of trying to adapt to international norms, why shouldn't we try to teach the world the Indian way of doing business?"[4]

Organizations in the West are only fairly recently coming to terms with the ongoing unpredictability of global markets and economies. India has had to deal with chaos and unpredictability for decades. Its approach to strategy, as a result, is highly proactive. The only way to succeed amid chaos is to stay one step beyond chaos. In contrast, Western corporate strategies are traditionally more reactive. Companies change tack when sales, profits, or stock prices are down; when there are new competitors; or when employees begin to leave. The trouble is that these are all trailing indicators. They are history. Indian companies have become adept at picking up leading indicators so that they can change strategies positively and proactively rather than defensively and reactively.

Over the course of decades working with companies in high-growth economies, including five years spent inside twenty Indian companies, I was able to come to understand the Indian approach to business strategy and to identify key lessons. Those lessons formed the basis for the Strategic Shock Absorbers in this book and guided my thinking around how they come together to form a complete discipline for operating through chaotic, shifting environments. I do not believe there is a single definitive Indian approach to strategy. Rather, Indian approaches to shaping and executing strategy share common elements that together add up to their own unique contribution to management innovation. As described in the last chapter, these elements are founded, first of all, on a compelling and ever-present sense of values.

Values Enable Coordination

In managing through complex, uncertain, high-speed change, it is critical that organizations have a common lens through which to interpret the changing environment. Otherwise, an organization will spend a great deal of time trying to establish a common context for understanding the problem, as opposed to solving it. For Indian companies, values provide that common lens. Values in the Indian context are not decorative adornments, but rather decision-making touchstones and reference points.

Of course, Indian companies do not have a monopoly on clearly articulated values to enable swift decision making and strategy formulation. Many Western companies, such as Google and Zappos, do recruit based on values, and they position values at center stage in decision making.

In India, values are traditionally the inescapable foundation of many organizations. They tend to be boldly and consistently articulated. At Welspun, their values are summed up in the statement "dare to commit." This is not pure gimmickry. Welspun has a history of making intrepid commitments to the customers and then going to great lengths to live up to them. They take values seriously. Likewise, in recent years Arvind Mills has undergone considerable change that has been guided by values. It labeled its more recent strategy, Renovision, "a new way of looking at issues, of seeing more than the obvious." Under this strategy, Arvind focused on serving the international markets. While this strategy was new, the values of delivering the best quality and continuous adaptation to the changing business environment remained constant, and that common lens is what enabled them to make Renovision work for them. It touched every aspect of the organization. Their factory was razed to the ground and a new one constructed. Their plant and machinery was entirely modernized at a time when most Indian mills would have made do with outdated or at least secondhand machinery to save costs.[5]

Other Indian companies place a similar premium on values. Future Group talks of "rewriting rules, retaining values." We saw that its Big Bazaar brand was one of the first Indian retailers to embrace hypermarket retailing. A guiding value of its model is Indianness, or remaining true to Indian culture and customs. Instead of replicating large Western-style stores, Big Bazaar recreates the traditional bazaar. This, along with on-the-ground learning and rewriting conventions, is what Future Group uses as a touchstone for each new retail concept and business strategy.

In practice, Welspun, Future Group, and other Indian companies use their values to implement their particular ways of working: an ability and willingness to absorb change without losing momentum; anticipating the future and seeing the external environment with clarity; executing accurately; and scanning and reacting with agility. The Indian model of management involves all four elements of the Strategic Shock Absorbers.

Absorbing Change without Losing Momentum

Being able to absorb change without losing momentum is a matter of focus and endurance. Indian companies have a willingness to take a hit and carry on, and this is increasingly necessary for all companies. As we have seen throughout this book, change is no longer linear, simple, or one-dimensional. Therefore, the ability of an enterprise to absorb chaos is a vital part of reaching its objectives. Conversely, resistance to change brings everything to a grinding halt.

We have seen that the capacity to absorb change has two key elements. First, there is a focus on the ends rather than the means. Strategy needs to be in service of achieving end goals as opposed to enforcing standardized processes. Second, the ability to absorb the unforeseen involves the creation of space for intellectual buffers.

Intellectual buffers seek to anticipate and absorb unforeseen events that could otherwise ambush the best strategies and most detailed plans. The excellence and appropriateness of a strategy is measured by its ability to deal with an imperfect world and an uncharted environment. Another way to build up intellectual slack is through an active brain trust. Almost every company I studied, alone or with colleagues, had a group of five to seven key people across the organization (not all senior executives) who would sit down at least once a week and think specifically about future changes in their business environment and how they would react to them. This innovation developed in India and the Middle East because a majority of businesses there were traditionally family owned. As the generations would sit down for dinner, business (both current activities as well as potential future changes) was one of the natural topics of conversation. With the introduction of professional managers, the brain trust was a way to continue having this conversation. It should be noted that in most businesses the brain trust blossoms over lunch!

I would argue that this active brain trust or intellectual buffer is one of the key innovations of strategic thinking that Indian companies bring. It is a coping mechanism that allows adaptation and yet enables companies to maintain stability in their core business. Moser Baer acknowledges that the active brain trust is one of the key adaptation mechanisms that allow them to keep up with potential changes in their business environment, yet maintain stable (Six Sigma) manufacturing processes in their base business.

Developing Foresight and Anticipating the Future

Foresight is alertness to the external world that assumes everything is in a constant state of change. With this foresight comes an understanding that strategies need to be continuously evaluated and updated. In Indian companies, changing course is seen not as failure on the part of strategy, but as a natural and positive part of a continuous process of strategy development and implementation. The implications of this are far reaching on the process of strategy development.

Two factors are particularly key. First, information must lead to the identification of a set of strategic assumptions, based on which particular strategy and implementation plan will be put together. This implies that if the assumptions change, the strategy changes too.

At Arvind Mills, strategic assumptions are constantly monitored. Each assumption factored into the company's strategic plan is monitored every day by its MIS department. According to Karthik Krishnan, chief manager for corporate strategy and projects:

> It is not only financial targets that mark a strategic plan. Every variant needs to be explained. In a typical plan for the coming year or a budget document of Arvind Mills, which is presented to the board, we state the assumptions. The budget assumptions talk about expected cotton prices in the coming year, market mixes in the various geographies, the critical accounts that will be cracked next year, and levels to which costs will be controlled. The budget view represents a consolidated budget projection built on a two separate cotton price scenarios: expected price range scenario and worst-case scenario. Any event that triggers a change in the assumptions will be brought up in the monthly reviews or at the time of occurrence of the event.

Second, exit strategies are as important as entry strategies. In other words, do not assume that your first (or second) strategy will work. Explicitly consider exit strategies and alternatives. This is critical in order to ensure that an initial plan does not land your organization in a strategic straitjacket from which it cannot free itself without huge expenditures of effort, time, and cost.

"When we try something new, which we are doing most of the time, there are bound to be some mistakes," says Damodar Mall, former group customer director of Future Group. "There could be some bets that we take, which do not reach fruition. However, if you are destroying what does not fit in your overall game plan; that helps you to have a strategically cleaner portfolio. So, rather than carrying the baggage, to clean your portfolio along the way is the smarter way to lead."

Air Deccan's strategy to pursue unexplored routes paid rich dividends. Very often, its precise selection of routes achieved high yields and high loads. The airline's presence on these routes, before other competitors, gave it an additional first-mover advantage. The carrier was aware that its success was dependent to a large extent on its load factor. Therefore, it discontinued routes after four months if load factor was found to be low. And when competition from other low-cost airlines intensified, Air Deccan was the first to read the signs. They enacted their profitable exit strategy in a sale to Kingfisher Airlines, extricating themselves before anyone else saw that market conditions were eroding.

Executing with Accuracy

India is a rush of people and of business coming from every conceivable direction. We've seen that to make a move successfully in this type of environment requires incredible accuracy. This applies internally as well as externally. The Indian companies I studied demonstrated that one of the fundamental elements of accuracy is for an organization to understand itself. In order to have quick decision making and immediate reactions to changing conditions, strategy must be transparent. This requires decision triggers.

Air Deccan came to see that its true competition was not other airlines (Indian Airlines, Jet Airways, and the like), but actually Indian Rail. From this, Air Deccan designed a very clear decision rule—find any route with a high percentage of first-class rail travelers that was underserved by airlines. Air Deccan attacked this opportunity and developed a cost structure so that air tickets would cost no more than a first-class rail ticket, while the time savings for customers were over 1,000 percent.

The other aspect of accuracy is what I have called forming the strategic wedge. Once an Indian company has a toehold with a particular client or in a particular industry it will seek to wedge itself deeper and deeper. It will take on more activities and expand to higher-value activities so that it becomes increasingly difficult for the client to change supplier.

Evalueserve's move into claims verification is one example of this type of move. Unlike a call center that performs relatively low-value or less complex tasks, Evalueserve employees are highly trained and perform research and financial analysis for investment companies. Doing some work for an insurance company, Evalueserve recognized the opportunity to move into medical claims and expanded their business accordingly in order to fill the void. It is in this way that Indian companies look for ways to turn small opportunities and openings into larger ones using a strategic wedge.

Reacting with Agility

Moving quickly in a crowd is second nature for Indians accustomed to chaotic, uncertain, and turbulent living and working environments. "It's hardwired in our genes to be able to work in a chaotically functioning society," says Sanjay Ray Chaudhuri, a director of Network18. "Everywhere you go, you see chaos; you see people thriving in chaos and you learn that to be ahead of the crowd you've got to be more unruly than the other guy because he won't stand quietly in the line."

Lessons learned from Indian companies indicate that agility requires three things happening consistently and simultaneously: a willing interaction with the environment; accurate processing of all available information; and the ability to make decisions and take actions based on these interactions and information. In the companies I studied, agility was displayed frequently as constant adaptation. Mahindra & Mahindra holds bona fide strategic planning meetings monthly. The others in my study each had their own ways of rapid strategy adaptation.

"No strategy can consistently keep through . . . years without changes. The market is very dynamic, and strategies have to be flexible," says Maheen Kannu of the logistics company Gati. Gati reviews strategy on a monthly, quarterly, half-yearly, and annual basis so that as the industry scenario changes it can modify its strategy accordingly.[6]

"Planning is a non-stop process," says Ramesh Sanka, chief financial officer of the real estate company DLF. "Over the last year, we have been adding to our holdings and at the same time selling some of our other interests. We have a strategic plan to achieve 50 million square feet every year but it could undergo a change. We are not bound to a number. According to the need of the hour, we may take this target higher or lower."[7]

Many of the elements of India's model of management are familiar to companies in the West. In the context of India, however, they come together to form an innovative discipline for surviving amid everyday chaos, embracing strategies that absorb shocks and converting them into positive change. These elements of strategy, and the accompanying management skills, form the foundation of a dynamic strategic planning process that is necessary for coping with a rapidly changing environment. Which of these elements are most critical to a firm depends on the firm's strategy as well as the overall conditions of industry competition. However, all elements are critical in order to increase the likelihood of long-term success. The speed at which these elements can be put in place and the depth of the capabilities supporting them will be fundamental elements of competitive success in the coming years as companies vie with each other in ever more rapidly changing and unpredictable environments.

Formalizing the Informal

The capabilities just described are geared to prepare companies to compete in the fast-moving markets that have become the norm everywhere. Part of the power they deliver is in how they bridge the formal and informal elements of strategic planning. Bringing both of these to the planning process is not new, but what is new and different is the manner in which the Strategic Shock Absorbers act as an adaptation and integration mechanism between the two. In many ways, the Strategic Shock Absorbers formalize the informal in order to clarify opportunities and accelerate change. Informal communication, ideation, and feedback are ongoing inside an organization; however, without these tools, ideas and expertise get lost or are very slow to filter up to senior management.

Each of the tools discussed in the book offers a different lens for bridging the formal and informal elements of strategy. The corporate concierge, for example, is a positive bottleneck that allows companies to systematically see *why* the external environment is changing. Strategic assumptions signal *when* you need to respond. An active think tank and exit strategies provide options for *how* to respond to changing competitive conditions. This is the unique value proposition of Strategic Shock Absorbers. They help organizations blend the formal and informal elements of strategy more effectively.

Without an approach such as this, harnessing the informal comes down to the art of management, pure and simple. My work with organizations in India and Dubai, however, revealed that iconic organizations in chaotic markets are accustomed to using certain techniques to make the strategic planning process more science and less art. Thus, Strategic Shock Absorbers represent a critical element in the evolution of management and strategy in terms of how organizations plan in frequently changing, turbulent, and increasingly unpredictable environments.

Figure 8.1 Integrate Formal and Informal Planning

Formalizing the informal . . .

✓ Uncovers opportunities.

✓ Accelerates change.

✓ Delivers intelligence.

✓ Clarifies priorities.

✓ Enhances communication.

✓ Bridges social networks and hierarchy.

A highly entrepreneurial organization by design, India's Network18[8] presents one of the more overt examples of explicitly balancing formal and informal strategic planning in order to remain agile and responsive. Owner and cofounder Raghav Bahl jumped into the industry when it was dominated by three entrenched players: the state-owned Doordarshan that enjoyed a monopoly until 1991, Rupert Murdoch's Star TV, and Subhash Chandra's Zee TV. In the early days of Network18, running a production company with some trusted partners offered no guarantee of cash flow in any given week. And when paid work *did* come along it was often difficult to find someone to do it. Sanjay Ray Chaudhuri, executive director and another cofounder, recalls how they put up a sign outside their offices announcing, "Trespassers will be hired!"[9]

Nonetheless, executives insist that employment was based on merit and their quality standards back up that assertion.

For example, at a point when the BBC was recognized as the epitome of quality programming, Network18 was the only Indian company to produce a show for them. As Network18 grew, the question foremost in Bahl's mind was always how to manage the trade-off between structure and entrepreneurial informality. And, by extension, how to ensure flexibility for Network18's young managers while making sure that they continue moving toward the same overarching corporate goal of the entire group.

Bahl told me, "We can't afford to be too planned." In an environment where one does not know when and what type of new opportunities may arise, he said that decision making needs to be extremely quick. If an organization is too structured, as is the case in conventional industries, opportunities may be lost. In addition, when the external environment can change halfway through an annual plan, the assumptions on which the plan was based may become redundant and render the plan invalid. Some estimates are required for planning, but in a new and unexplored market the data points may not yet be available for number crunching.

Network18 is an organization that cherishes its culture and employee commitment as the most important risk-management tools it has. Strategic planning has been more about finding people they trust to lead than creating the "best-laid plans." Planning, systems, and processes exist but are sparse compared even to more traditional Indian businesses. Upon being asked about structure for long-term direction and new ventures, Bahl comments candidly, "Much as I would like to say that we are structured about it, I don't think we always are. I think a lot of our decisions are gut-feel oriented. We cannot afford to be too planned in our business because who knows where the next opportunity comes from?"[10]

Group CFO RDS Bawa acknowledges changes have taken place more recently to reflect an increasing emphasis on structure at Network18: "As we have grown, we have put more processes into place. We interact more with the market." But their balance between formal and informal planning still comes down to this—hire the best and most-trusted people, instill common values and quality standards, and provide latitude in terms of decisions.[11]

Today, the station owns India's leading English and Hindi business news channels, as well as India's leading English general news channel, and India's leading business news and general news websites.

A large part of the informality at Network18 comes from the news industry dynamic, to be sure. The common view across the organization is that a journalist cannot wait for formal reviews and instructions or approvals when he or she is breaking news of, say, a natural disaster. Although this is just one example, it is a good indicator of the type of industry environment where reflexes are important and reaction time is counted in seconds.

Industry environment aside, the balance between formal and informal planning was evident in every Indian company I worked with, bar none; and each used it to improve their response time and make better decisions.

Moser Baer, for example, operates in a high-tech environment with formal quality measures and Six Sigma manufacturing, creating a situation where the process has to be very controlled. Yet, at the same time, there is a degree of informality intentionally built into the processes. Vivek Chaturvedi, from Moser Baer Solar, explains how they manage to allow for flexibility: "While planning requires regiments and having things in place, in India we thrive on enabling last minute changes and keeping everything open and flexible right to the 11th hour ... and there are about 24 11th hours in India in a day."[12]

At Moser Baer, executives told me about a tradition of involving the entire organization in planning. In particular, they believe in the importance of information exchanged through informal channels. When strategic planning is conducted at Moser in a top-down way, everybody throughout the organization is provided with the full background, rationale, and details of any new plan or system. They find that the dissemination of information through formal and informal channels helps lessen the resistance to change.

Arvind Mills had similar things to say. According to Ajit Mantagani, the CEO of their denim business, the types of major changes they have made over the years are a result of "informal interaction and informal communication over a period of time."[13] He said that they intentionally cultivate informal interactions. At the same time, Mantagani does not discount formal meetings and professional teams for guiding the process. Any conflict between formal and informal planning processes at Arvind Mills, he said, is resolved through different methods, including debate between formal and informal groups, influence exerted by each group over each other, and resting of decision-making authority in a person higher up the chain of command. The opinion of the formal decision-making group may also be influenced through the informal process. For instance, after a sales manager visits clients, apart from their formal report they also pass along informal feedback. This informal feedback plays its own part in influencing the opinion of the members of the formal group who make decisions about matters such as product development.

In fact, the informal planning process at Arvind Mills takes place simultaneously with formal planning. The informal plays the role of a forum for discussion. It is through informal discussions that qualitative ideas are considered and candid observations about a situation can be communicated. This qualitative interchange is important because turbulent environments imply that sufficient data may not be available for making decisions based on quantitative evidence.

In several organizations I worked with, the balance between formal and informal focused heavily on creating more structure, as opposed to less. At Future Group, for example, innovation tended to happen in a more informal way with little structure. Yet, because it is such an important element in their success, they chose to slide the scale to make it *more* formal by creating a C-suite position—CEO of Innovation and Incubation. This sent a signal to the organization that innovation was a top priority. At the same time, it created a semirigid structure in order to earmark resources without stifling the type of innovation that was happening as a matter of course.

Ayurvedic medicine manufacturer Dabur chose a similar path by creating a chief risk officer (CRO). Each employee at Dabur is encouraged to identify risk and report it to the concerned risk officer who then reports it to the CRO.

According to Byas Anand, senior manager of corporate communications, the move was intended to formalize and enhance risk management at Dabur and achieve greater internal control without stifling individual responsibility.

At NDTV, the culture is inclined toward informal communication, and yet the company has adopted a more structured approach toward planning and decision making. In fact, the balance between the two is something they put considerable effort into. There are three main levels of decision making at NDTV—board of directors, group CEO and chairman, and CEOs and managing editors. The board of directors plays a formal role in the planning and strategy process. It is not expected to be involved in operational decision making. The board usually reviews the quarterly financial reports and annual results. Informal channels of communication with the board are limited.

Between the CEOs and managing editors and the group CEO and chairman, however, a substantial volume of communication is informal. Such communication is a part of decision making as well as for updating the group CEO or chairman with critical information on a weekly basis. Formal channels are used only on formal occasions such as the monthly or quarterly review of balance sheets. Most of the decisions are made informally. Between the functional heads and the CEOs also, there is a significant volume of informal communication. Most of the operational information and decisions are conveyed over the phone and via e-mails or during informal meetings. However, formal meetings are called for if there is a major issue to be tackled.

According to Prannoy Lal Roy, NDTV's cofounder, "We would like to retain the ease and flexibility of informal communication, while improving our formal system of communication. We reconcile the two in a very unique way. We identify informal groups being formed in the organization. For instance, heads of distribution, HR, finance, sales and marketing and the CEOs often work very closely. We empower these informal groups to communicate with each other in order to speed-up the process of decision making. We bring them closer to each other through company-sponsored parties and get-togethers. This helps them to work as a team."[14]

Managing the interplay between formal and informal planning and communication is one of the primary fulcrums that executives in India use to make their uniquely agile and responsive management style work. What is important to point out here is that in most cases this balancing act is intentional. They are formalizing the informal in order to accelerate decision making and enable greater flexibility in an environment of constant change.

This Indian management mode is characterized by a few primary elements.

First, Indian companies act fast and remain alert and fluid by honing the capabilities within the four Strategic Shock Absorbers. Nearly all of the companies I studied use every or nearly every tool described throughout this book. These are the specific means by which they have been able to thrive through ongoing change and chaos. These capabilities are the same ones that any organization anywhere can use to absorb the impact of unexpected events without slowing down or destabilizing the entire organization.

Next, we've seen that values are the one immovable force on which individuals can rely to gain their bearings and establish a clear basis for making good decisions, even when everything else around them is shifting.

Finally, people are the ultimate competitive advantage. As we have talked about throughout this book, the art of management is something that requires personal judgment. We know from chemistry that the same few chemicals can create either a perfect solution or a massive explosion—it just depends upon how they are mixed together by the chemist.

The advice in this book (and the lessons from India and Dubai) will make a positive difference only if individual leaders put a stake in the ground and make an effort to customize the approach to suit their own business. On a personal level, this requires asking the question: *what type of leader do I want to be?* Abandoning the old mode of strategic planning requires the courage to adopt a new gestalt. It may appear risky, but the bigger risk is in *not* pushing against the norm and choosing to remain the same. What I hope is that this book, with its advice and many examples, will aid you along your own journey to develop Strategic Shock Absorbers as you adapt to the turbulent world that all of us are facing.

Notes

Introduction

1. Rupert Neate, "Kodak Falls in the 'Creative Destruction of the Digital Age,'" *The Guardian*, Jan. 19, 2012, http://www.theguardian.com/business /2012/jan/19/kodak-bankruptcy-protection.

2. International Monetary Fund, *World Economic Outlook—Recovery Strengthens, Remains Uneven*, Washington, April 2014, 2, http://www.imf.org /external/pubs/ft/weo/2014/01/pdf/text.pdf.

3. The World Bank, "GDP Growth (Annual %)," Worldbank.org, http://data.worldbank.org/indicator/NY.GDP.MKTP.KD.ZG/countries (accessed May 12, 2014).

4. The material in this example, including quotations and data, is drawn from the author's case study. Whenever possible, the data has been updated with the latest available figures. Jeffrey Sampler, *Thriving in a Turbulent Environment Case Study: DLF*, 2008, 8.

5. Dabur Company, *Annual Report*, FY 2007.

6. Ibid.

7. Ibid.

8. Jeffrey Sampler, *Thriving in a Turbulent Environment Case Study: Arvind Mills Ltd.*, July 2007.

9. Sampler, *Case Study: DLF*, 10.

Chapter 1

1. The material in this example, including quotations and data, is drawn from the author's case study. Whenever possible, the data has been updated with the latest available figures. Jeffrey Sampler, *Thriving in a Turbulent Environment Case Study: Gati Limited*, Aug. 2007, 9.
2. Ibid., 14.

Chapter 2

1. Jason Daley, "How Pizza Hut Made a Comeback," *Entrepreneur*, Dec. 14, 2011, http://www.entrepreneur.com/article/222411.
2. Technomic, Inc., "Pizza Chains Succeed in Slow Economy through Focused Positioning, Reports Technomic," press release, *Businesswire*, Sept. 24, 2009, http://www.businesswire.com/news/home/20090924005 604/en/Pizza-Chains-Succeed-Slow-Economy-Focused-Positioning# .U3IqKfldVqU.
3. "Hot, Fast and Engaged," *Chief Marketer*, June 1, 2010, http://www.chief marketer.com/special-reports-chief-marketer/hot-fast-and-engaged-01062010.
4. Sampler, *Case Study: DLF*, 1.
5. Ibid., 6.
6. The material in this example, including quotations and data, is drawn from the author's case study. Whenever possible, the data has been updated with the latest available figures. Jeffrey Sampler, *Air Deccan, Case Study*, (Massachusetts Institute of Technology, Nov. 2006), CISR Working Paper 365 and MIT Sloan Working Paper 4657–07, http: //dspace.mit.edu/bitstream/handle/1721.1/39807/4657–07.pdf?sequen.
7. Directorate General of Civil Aviation, Government of India, *Centre for Monitoring Indian Economy Monthly Economic Indicator*, Nov. 2005.
8. Centre for Aviation, "Story of Exceptional Growth in Indian Domestic Market Takes Diversion," centreforaviation.com, http://centrefor aviation.com/analysis/story-of-exceptional-growth-in-indian-domestic-market-takes-diversion-80474 (accessed May 14, 2014).
9. Vanik: Leading Institute for Banking and Railway, "Railway in India," vanik.org, http://vanik.org/railway_india.php (accessed May 18, 2014).

10. Sampler, *Air Deccan*, 3.

11. Ibid., 7.

12. Ibid.

13. Ibid., 14.

14. Ruth David, "Kingfisher Buys Stake in Air Deccan," *Forbes*, June 1, 2007, http://www.forbes.com/2007/06/01/kingfisher-deccan-tieup-markets-equity-cx_rd_0601markets2.html.

15. Jeffrey Sampler and Saeb Eigner, *Sand to Silicon* (London: Profile Books, 2003).

16. Sampler, *Case Study: Gati Limited*, 14.

17. Lily Hayyes-Kaufman, "Wal-Mart's Backward Business Revolution," *Forbes*, Aug. 11, 2009, http://www.forbes.com/2009/08/10/wal-mart-business-strategy-labor-opinions-book-review-wal-mart.html.

18. Associated Press, "How Gillette Execs Spent a Fortune Developing a Razor for India Using MIT Student Focus Groups . . . without Considering the Country's Lack of Running Water," *Mailonline*, Oct. 3, 2013, http://www.dailymail.co.uk/news/article-2443191/Gillette-spent-fortune-Indian-razor-forgetting-countrys-running-water.html.

19. Ibid.

20. Jaiswal Kamya, "Can Gillette Tap into Rural Market and Yet Retain Its Value for Urban Consumers?" *The Economic Times India*, Dec. 11, 2011, http://articles.economictimes.indiatimes.com/2011–12–11/news/3050 2422_1_razor-and-blade-gillette-india-mach.

21. Ibid.

22. Sampler, *Air Deccan*, 39.

Chapter 3

1. Stephen Armstrong, "The Son of a Railwayman Who Launched a Runaway Chain," *Telegraph.co.uk*, Aug. 13, 2008, http://fashion.telegraph.co.uk/news-features/TMG3365113/The-son-of-a-railwayman-who-launched-a-runaway-chain.html.

2. Suzy Hansen, "How Zara Grew into the World's Largest Fashion Retailer," *New York Times*, Nov. 9, 2012, http://www.nytimes.com/2012

/11/11/magazine/how-zara-grew-into-the-worlds-largest-fashion-retailer.html?pagewanted=all&_r=0.

3. Sarah Morris, "Zara Owner Inditex Sidesteps European Gloom," *Reuters UK*, March 13, 2013, http://uk.reuters.com/article/2013/03/13/uk-inditex-idUKBRE92C07G20130313.

4. Jeffrey Sampler, *Case Study: Arvind Mills*, 12.

5. Ibid., 13.

6. Ibid.

7. Ibid., 14.

8. The quotation is from my case study interviews with Moser Baer executives for the case: Jeffrey Sampler, *Thriving in a Turbulent Environment Case Study: Moser Baer*, 2008.

9. Hansen, "How Zara Grew," *New York Times*.

10. Cheche V. Moral, "Meet the Charles and Keith behind Charles & Keith," *Philippine Daily Inquirer*, Sept. 6, 2013, http://www.inquirer.net/travel-philippines/articles?pid=123841&chan=8.

11. The World Bank, "GDP Growth (Annual %)," http://data.worldbank.org/indicator/NY.GDP.MKTP.KD.ZG/countries (accessed May 15, 2014).

12. Ibid.

13. International Business Publications, *United Arab Emirates: How to Invest, Start and Run a Profitable Business in the UAE Guide*, 36. (Updated annually. Accessed May 14, 2014), http://books.google.com/books?id=JldwAwAAQBAJ&pg=PA36&lpg=PA36&dq=international+herald+tribune+value+of+dubai%27s+economy+in+2006&source=bl&ots=xyFxn2JDPj&sig=8p8vpG_ZgJ8p2YpjWnQ1tdyo4t8&hl=en&sa=X&ei=4mlzU-ivEuLfsASKkID4Ag&ved=0CC0Q6AEwAQ#v=onepage&q=international%20herald%20tribune%20value%20of%20dubai's%20economy%20in%202006&f=false.

14. Sampler and Eigner, *Sand to Silicon*, 135.

15. Ibid.

16. The material in this example, including quotations and data, is drawn from the author's case study. Whenever possible, the data has been

updated with the latest available figures. Jeffrey Sampler, *Thriving in a Turbulent Environment Case Study: Gati Limited*, Aug. 2007.

17. Ibid., 10.

18. Ibid., 13.

19. Hoovers, Inc., "Gati Limited," *Hoovers.com*, http://hoovweb.hoovers .com/company/GATI_LIMITED/rkhrcyi-1–1njht4–1njhft.html (accessed May 14, 2014).

20. Gulf Oil & Gas, "Total to Buy ExxonMobil's Downstream Interests in 14 African Countries," *gulfoilandgas.com*, Sept. 5, 2005, http://www .gulfoilandgas.com/webpro1/MAIN/Mainnews.asp?id=1734.

21. Total S.A., *The Shareholders Newsletter Report: The New Exploration Frontiers*, Spring 2012, 2, http://total.com/en/total-shareholders-newsletter-39.

22. Andrew E. Kramer, "Kazakhstan Oil Field Begins Production after Years of Delay," *New York Times*, Sept. 11, 2013, http://www.nytimes .com/2013/09/12/business/global/kazakhstan-oil-field-starts-production-after-years-of-delay.html.

23. Sampler, *Case Study: DLF*, 12.

24. The material in this example, including quotations and data, is drawn from the author's case study. Whenever possible, the data has been updated with the latest available figures. Jeffrey Sampler, *Thriving in a Turbulent Environment Case Study: Welspun India*, July 2007, 11.

25. Ibid., 12.

26. Ibid.

27. Ibid.

28. Tony Hsieh, "How I Did It: Zappos's CEO on Going to Extremes for Customers," *Harvard Business Review*, July 2010, http://hbr.org/2010/07 /how-i-did-it-zapposs-ceo-on-going-to-extremes-for-customers/ar/1.

29. Sampler, *Case Study: Arvind Mills*, 14.

Chapter 4

1. James Surowiecki, "The Next Level," *The New Yorker*, Oct. 18, 2010. http://www.newyorker.com/talk/financial/2010/10/18/101018ta_talk_ surowiecki.

2. Greg Sandoval, "Netflix's Lost Year: The Inside Story of the Price-Hike Train Wreck," *CNET.com*, July 11, 2012. http://www.cnet.com/news/netflixs-lost-year-the-inside-story-of-the-price-hike-train-wreck/.

3. The material in this example, including quotations and data, is drawn from the author's case study. Whenever possible, the data has been updated with the latest available figures. Some of this material was also published in *The Smart Manager*, Nov-Dec. 2010. Jeffrey Sampler, *Thriving in a Turbulent Environment Case Study: Future Group*, Apr. 2007.

4. Future Group, "Retail: Winning the Hearts of Indian Consumers," *futuregroup.in/index.aspx*, http://www.futuregroup.in/businesses/modern-retail.html (accessed May 15, 2014).

5. Sampler, *Case Study: Future Group*, 4.

6. Ibid., 11.

7. Ibid.

8. Ibid., 11–12.

9. Ibid., 12.

10. Ibid.

11. Future Group, "Future Group Advantage: Let's Have Fun Together," *futuregroup.in/index.aspx*, http://www.futuregroup.in/careers/future-group-advantage.html (accessed May 15, 2014).

12. Sampler, *Case Study: Future Group*, 16.

13. The material in this example, including quotations and data, is drawn from the author's case study. Whenever possible, the data has been updated with the latest available figures. Jeffrey Sampler, *Thriving in a Turbulent Environment Case Study: Dabur*, 2008.

14. Ibid., 17.

15. Sampler, *Case Study: Arvind Mills*, 20.

16. Sampler, *Case Study: Network18*, 22.

17. Sampler, *Case Study: Arvind Mills*, 14.

18. Sampler, *Case Study: Gati Limited*, 12.

19. The material in this example, including quotations and data, is drawn from the author's case study. Whenever possible, the data has been updated with the latest available figures. Some of this material was also

published in *The Smart Manager*, Nov-Dec. 2010. Jeffrey Sampler, *Thriving in a Turbulent Environment Case Study: Moser Baer*, 2008.

20. Sampler, *Case Study: Gati Limited*, 13.

Chapter 5

1. The material in this example, including quotations and data, is drawn from the author's case study. Whenever possible, the data has been updated with the latest available figures. Some of this material was also published in *The Smart Manager*, Nov-Dec. 2010. Jeffrey Sampler, *Thriving in a Turbulent Environment Case Study: Arvind Mills Ltd*, July 2007.

2. Sampler, *Case Study: DLF*, 6.

3. The material in this example, including quotations and data, is drawn from the author's case study. Whenever possible, the data has been updated with the latest available figures. Jeffrey Sampler, *Thriving in a Turbulent Environment Case Study: Evalueserve*, Apr. 2006.

4. Evalueserve, "Our Company," evalueserve.com, http://www.evalueserve .com/about-us/our-company/ (accessed May 18, 2014).

5. "DLF: A Ready Reckoner," *India Today*, Oct. 10, 2012, http://indiatoday .intoday.in/story/dlf-a-ready-reckoner/1/224176.html.

6. Sampler, *Case Study: DLF*, 10.

7. Sampler, *Case Study: Arvind Mills*, 2.

8. Ibid., 11.

Chapter 6

1. Kelly Kennedy, "CVS Calls It Quits: No More Tobacco Products," *USA Today*, Feb. 6, 2014, http://www.usatoday.com/story/news/nation/2014 /02/05/cvs-will-no-longer-sell-tobacco-products/5207853/.

2. Sampler, *Case Study: DLF*, 1.

3. PTI, "DLF Office Leasing Up 50% in FY14 to 3 Million Square Feet," *Economic Times*, April 24, 2014. http://economictimes.indiatimes.com /articleshow/34123971.cms?utm_source=contentofinterest&utm_ medium=text&utm_campaign=cppst.

4. "DLF Profile," *Forbes*, http://www.forbes.com/companies/dlf/ (accessed May 16, 2014).

5. Sampler, *Case Study: DLF,* 7.

6. From author interviews with DLF executives for Sampler, *Case Study: DLF.*

7. Sampler, *Case Study: DLF,* 4.

8. Ibid., 3.

9. Ibid., 10.

10. Ibid., 11.

11. Ibid., 12

12. Ibid., 15.

13. Ibid.

14. Ibid., 18.

Chapter 7

1. Sampler, *Case Study: Future Group*, 12.

2. Sampler, *Case Study: Arvind Mills.*

3. Arvind, "Arvind: Our People," Arvind.com, http://www.arvind.com/company/people.htm (accessed May 16, 2014).

4. Sampler, *Case Study: Arvind Mills,* 9.

5. Ibid.

6. Ibid.

7. Sampler, *Case Study: Evalueserve,* 14.

8. Ibid., 12.

9. The material in this example, including quotations and data, is drawn from the author's case study. Whenever possible, the data has been updated with the latest available figures. Jeffrey Sampler, *Thriving in a Turbulent Environment Case Study: NDTV,* Aug. 2007.

10. Ibid., 2.

11. Ibid., 3.

12. Ibid., 7.

13. Ibid., 9.

14. Ibid.

15. Ibid., 9–10.

16. The World Bank, "GDP Growth (Annual %)" http://data.worldbank.org/indicator/NY.GDP.MKTP.KD.ZG/countries (accessed May 17, 2014).

17. Sampler, *Case Study: Gati*, 18.

18. Ibid.

19. Hoovers, Inc., "Gati Limited," *Hoovers.com*; Gati, "Gati Ltd's Q1 FY14 Consolidated YoY Total Income Rises 22 Percent and QoQ Income Rises 12 Percent to Rs. 367 Crore," press release, *gati.com*, Nov. 6, 2013, http://www.gati.com/images/pdf/media-center/press-release/Q1FY14-FINAL.pdf.

20. http://www.gati.com/images/pdf/investors/financial-reports/concall-transcripts/GATI-Q2FY14-Concall-Transcript.pdf.

21. Sampler, *Case Study: Moser Baer*, 16.

22. Ibid.

23. "The Technology Manufacturer," *Industry.2.0*, June 2005, 53. http://www.moserbaer.com/images/media_coverage/technologymanufacturer.pdf.

Chapter 8

1. Some of the material in this chapter was adapted from an article cowritten by the author based on the author's cases. Jeffrey Sampler and Sanjeev Sarkar, "Surviving India: Developing Strategic Shock Absorbers," *The Smart Manager*, Nov-Dec. 2010, 15. http://thesmartmanager.com/file/021210462303_TheSmartManager,_SpecialFeature,_SurvivingIndia,_JeffreySampler,_Nov-Dec-10.pdf.

2. Arvind, "Arvind to Be Rs. 2000 Cr Brand in 5 Years," press release, *arvind.com*, June 13, 2013, http://www.arvind.com/pdf/shareholding/2014/Press%20Release%207.6.2013.pdf.

3. Infosys, "History," infosys.com, http://www.infosys.com/about/Pages/history.aspx (accessed May 18, 2014).

4. Sampler, *Case Study: Moser Baer*, 23.

5. Sampler, *Case Study: Arvind Mills*, 8.

6. Sampler, *Case Study: Gati*, 14.

7. Sampler, *Case Study: DLF*, 7.

8. The material in this example, including quotations and data, is drawn from the author's case study. Jeffrey Sampler, *Thriving in a Turbulent Environment Case Study: Network18*. Whenever possible, the data has

been updated with the latest available figures. Some of this material was also published in *The Smart Manager*, Nov-Dec. 2010, by Jeffrey Sampler.

9. Quotation is taken from my own case interviews.

10. Quotation is taken from my own case interviews.

11. Quotation is taken from my own case interviews.

12. Sampler, *Case Study: Moser Baer*, 18.

13. Sampler, *Case Study: Arvind Mills*, 8.

14. Sampler, *Case Study: NDTV*, 14.

The Author

Jeffrey Sampler is an adjunct professor of strategy and technology at China Europe International Business School (CEIBS). Previously he was a faculty member of London Business School and the University of Oxford for over twenty years. His research interests include the strategic implications of new technology and the management of information as a strategic resource. His work has appeared in such journals as *Accounting, Management, and Information Technology*; *Fortune Journal of Management Studies*; *Journal of Management Information Systems*; *MIS Quarterly*; *Sloan Management Review*; and *Strategic Management Journal*. He has written two books on the economic transformation of Dubai, *Sand to Silicon* and *Sand to Silicon—Going Global*.

Dr. Sampler is also a frequent speaker at conferences and corporate management retreats and has traveled over 2.5 million miles to give lectures in over thirty-five countries. He has advised and been a board member of both FTSE 100 corporations and start-ups, as well as advising two heads of state. In addition, he has extensive experience advising family businesses and has worked with top family groups in India and Thailand for many years. He also has been featured in *Newsweek, BBC Television, BBC World Service, BBC Radio, CNBC, Economic Times,* and *Financial Mail.*

Index